Evaluation of penal measures

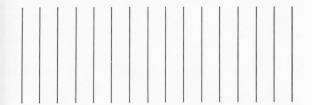

LESLIE T. WILKINS

UNIVERSITY OF CALIFORNIA • *Berkeley*

Consulting editor: *Leonard Savitz* . Temple University

Evaluation of

RANDOM HOUSE •

penal measures

NEW YORK

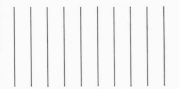

Preface

All types of people are doing all sorts of things to all types of persons, always with the belief that they are doing them good or thereby in some other way improving society.

But are they?

How do we know?

What is the value of rehabilitative techniques used in prisons, probation, community treatment, or the like? Is the general public getting value for the tax money which is being spent by all the professional agencies concerned with the many aspects of social control and personal problems?

This book examines the problems of evaluation with particular reference to penal measures, although the techniques of analysis and the logic of inference required in this sector do not differ significantly from those needed to answer similar questions in other areas of social action and policy.

This book is intended to appeal to those in universities and state colleges who are concerned with the teaching of undergraduates in the fields of law, social work, criminology, and related disciplines of social science and philosophy. It is also intended to provide guidance for the administrator at the state or local level who wishes to assess the efficiency of the operations of his agency.

No prior knowledge in the social sciences is assumed on the part of the reader.

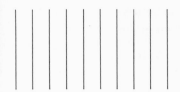

Contents

XI   CONTENTS

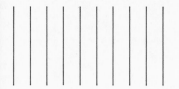

Evaluation of penal measures

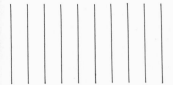

Introduction

Ask the average laymen what ought to be done with thieves, drug addicts, sexual deviants, and other offenders, and it is almost certain that they will reply with a considerable degree of assurance. While each person questioned may be confident that he is right, the concordance among various answers will be no more than coincidental. Ask an expert in the field of criminology or corrections the same questions, and he will be less certain. Ask the layman what types of treatment for offenders are likely to be more effective in prevention of further crimes, and it may be expected that his answers will be very similar to those he gave to the previous question. But these two questions are of different kinds. The first type includes the word "ought" and raises a moral question; the second raises a question of effectiveness in reference to the degree that the implied objective of crime prevention is attained by different means.

EFFECTIVENESS

What may be right in a moral sense may not be effective. What is effective for a stated purpose may be assessed by scientific methods, but these methods are not concerned with what may be morally appropriate. Some would see the moral aspects of the treatment of offenders as supreme; others would consider that even the moral aspects of treatment cannot be discussed in any satisfactory way without some prior assessment of the effectiveness of the systems used to reach an objective.

If we consider that the death penalty is a moral necessity for murder, there is no data which can further inform us; our belief that an eye for an eye and a life for a life is an essential feature of a moral system cannot be touched by scientific evidence unless we are prepared to make further statements in support of our belief. If we seek to support this belief by stating that the existence of the death penalty deters others from committing murder, this statement takes us out of the completely moral field, and it becomes possible to see how information may be supplied to throw light on such a statement. If we believe that all violent offenders should, as a moral necessity, be punished by corporal punishment, again we would be supporting a belief to which no further evidence could be relevant. As soon as we seek to support this belief by extensions of the statement, we may be entering upon a position where information can become relevant.

In practice, information impinges upon most of our value judgments. It is reasonably certain that most persons would take a different "moral" view if one of the following situations applied to corporal punishment. Let us suppose that information is available to support either of two opposite cases:

1. All violent offenders subjected to corporal punishment commit further crimes.
2. All violent offenders subjected to corporal punishment commit no further crimes.

Not many persons would maintain exactly the same moral views about corporal punishment in each of these cases. Of course, neither of the two extreme cases represents the known situation, but the relationship between information and moral decisions may be taken as demonstrated. If we can conceive of a modification of a moral judgment under two widely different sets of information, is it not reasonable to assume that in the less extreme case there may be a less extreme impact? At what point can we conceive of the information as being so trivial that it has no impact? Perhaps only at the point when information itself becomes trivial.

We do not propose to discuss whether it is morally right to seek the attainment of effectiveness in the systems for treatment of offenders. It is possible, and it seems desirable, however, to ask what is known about the effectiveness of each of the various ways in which modern society deals with its offenders. These questions can be attacked without reference to moral issues as such. When more is known about ways in which effectiveness can be assessed, it may be necessary to reexamine some of the issues presently being discussed in ethical terms. Perhaps moral objections may be sustained to some of the methods that might be proposed for increasing our knowledge of levels of effectiveness. Again, this is a valid but separate issue. Only one moral problem arises at this stage. Should we seek information concerning what we may regard as effective? Would it in any sense be more moral not to seek to inquire?

That evildoing should be punished is an idea which has been with us for a long time. The idea of efficacy in relation to social-control systems is much more recent. Often these two distinct elements are confounded. What is believed to be right morally is believed to be more effective. This is not necessarily true, nor is it necessarily false. Most moral philosophers, pioneers in psychology and psychiatry, religious apologists, and many others have commented on the concept of punishment. It is only recently that the concept of treatment has been introduced in relation to criminal behavior, but this too is attracting comment from a wide variety of sources. To select any particular authority (from the Bible or earlier documents to the present day) or to contrast the ideas of different authorities would not help to achieve our purposes in this book. We are not concerned here with the wide variety of ideas or with the backgrounds of persons who held or hold these views, but rather with the means for assessing the outcome from the application of concepts, whatever form they may take. However, it is appropriate to note the work of Beccaria [1738–1794] who in an essay on *Crime and Punishment* (8), published in 1809, discussed ideas relating to probability and measurement in relation to law and the maintenance of law and order. For example (page 80), he remarks: "Crimes are more effectively prevented by the *certainty* than the *severity* of punishment." But by "certainty" he apparently meant the degrees of certainty, because earlier (page 46) he says:

It may seem extraordinary that I speak of probability with regard to crimes, which, to deserve punishment, must be certain. But this paradox will vanish when it is considered, that, strictly speaking, moral certainty is only probability.

His ideas on the "proportion between crimes and punishments" are related to what he calls "political arithmetic" and "a calculation of probabilities to mathematical exactness." "If," he says, "mathematical calculations could be applied to the obscure and infinite combinations of human actions, there might be a corresponding scale of punishments, descending from the greatest to the least. . . ." Elsewhere he says: "there ought to be a fixed proportion between crimes and punishments." But he also maintained that "every individual [is] bound to society, [and] society is equally bound to him, by a contract which, from its nature equally binds both parties." His view was uncomplicated by concepts of "treatment" and related to the joint purpose of deterrence (general prevention) and punishment for the crime according to the nature of the crime. But he saw no inconsistency between this view and the opinion that "all punishments which exceed the necessity of preserving this bond [between society and the individual] are in their nature unjust."

Research has not yet been able to show the contribution toward social integration that is afforded by crime and its treatment or punishment. Criminologists now generally agree that the death penalty for murder does not deter murderers, even though it affords certainty that there is no recidivism! The calculus of probabilities has not been applied to the punishment of offenders, and the early interest in this approach (noted above) was soon replaced by a humanitarian philosophy. Emotional appeals for reform, supported by novelists, Quakers, and many others, became more prevalent. But we will proceed to the assessment of the practical consequences that result from the application of various theories.

THE HUMANITARIAN APPROACH

One result of recent research in the criminological field may be stated here: Insofar as the reform of offenders is concerned, there is already much hard evidence to show that what is generally regarded as humanitarian (or even "lenient") treatment of offenders is *at least* as effective as severe punishment or lengthy imprisonment. This is not to say that in any general way humanitarian treatments have been proved more effective *because* they are humanitarian. There is no reason to be ashamed of seeking to humanize social-control systems on moral grounds, but when a claim is made that because it is more humane it must be more effective, the enthusiasm of the humanitarian has exceeded reasonable bounds. This enthusiasm may sometimes lead to a situation that cannot be defended, with resulting damage to the cause of both the scientist and the humanitarian.

Much has been claimed for the reforming power of institutions of treatment, from probation to short, sharp shock, and from group therapy to the inculcation of habits of industry. ("Short, sharp shock" is a period of disciplinary training for young offenders, usually three months, in institutions having medium security provisions and located in England and Wales, called Detention Centres.) But research to date has not revealed very striking differences between methods, insofar as they can be distinguished by subsequent reconvictions of the offenders concerned. The human being is highly resistant to change. This is functional, no matter what the direction of change. Fortunately, it is not easy to change personality. If it were possible to change offenders from "bad" to "good" without much effort, changes from "good" to "bad" could probably be effected as simply and perhaps would involve a larger proportion of the population.

There seems to be some danger in some quarters at the present to undervalue the humanitarian aspect in penal treatment. It is possible that in some countries authorities might be self-satisfied with their treatment of offenders in prisons and other correctional establishments. They may view treatment as so therapeutic and resocializing that they may underrate the effect of incarceration and deprivation of liberty and the concomitant loss of communication links with society which even the inmates of the so-called ideal prisons must experience. Certainly in those countries where the prisons are considered modern and treatment-oriented, the incarceration rates tend to be extremely high, due mainly to lengthy periods of confinement.

If effective treatment requires a long period of institutional confinement, so too does severe punishment. But treatment, as the term is currently applied, implies a different dimension than punishment. Is there not, perhaps, some confounding of the two concepts in our current thought? Would it not be more efficient if we could separate the two dimensions, at least for purposes of discussing the objectives of the penal system? It is this that this book attempts to do by discussing aspects of rational decision processes and the concept of efficacy and its measurement.

The reader may consider his own ethical stand in relation to the issues as presented here. No moral viewpoint will be presented, but the relevance of moral concepts cannot be completely avoided.

TECHNOLOGY AND SOCIAL ACTION

People-changing is a rather peculiar business in which to be. Engineering, chemistry, and even medical science mainly consist of knowledge of a different order from that which forms the content of most social science. The former types of knowledge are invariant under different conditions and are not influenced by the social setting, while human science is variant under different conditions. To what extent the results of research in one country may be safely assumed to apply in another depends upon the type of knowledge. Technologies may be copied and adapted in different cultures, but the impact of technological changes will differ as much as the cultures differ.

There is, as yet, little of technology in the social-work field. For example, the techniques of probation do not form a universal basis for dealing with offenders. The bases of evaluating technology and social-action factors must be differentiated.

The differences between a magic love potion or another folk remedy for any ill or evil and modern medical drugs are not to be found in differences in their chemical compositions as such. Only in the relationship between the chemical composition and the other relevant information can the differences be found. In other words,

the one dimension of information (chemistry) is not of itself adequate to provide an assessment of the medicine that will satisfy a
rational man in the twentieth century.

It is a surprising and perhaps even shocking fact that our present-
day society is engaged in many activities which have no more support in terms of reliable evidence than the incantations of medicine
men and the potions of witches. The arguments used by many
highly placed and respected persons to support these activities are
similar to those which might be used to defend any other supersti-
tion. Is the treatment of offenders such an activity? To answer this
question, we must discuss the logical basis for inference, because
this is the basis upon which we reject any tendency we may have
to believe in witches, love potions, or other magic formulas of the
past or present.

It is time for us to pause and examine the bases of our assumed
knowledge and beliefs in the field of penology. Perhaps where we
know so little we should not be anxious to try to do so much. Have
we been overactive on the basis of too little knowledge? Spinoza
noted this danger when he remarked: "He who tries to determine
everything by law will foment crime rather than lessen it."

There is a danger of encapsulating philosophies and systems into
rules and laws and into prisons, with the result that the development of society's informal social controls is inhibited. The trend
toward the use of formal legal systems as the main means of social
control in mass societies may not be a trend in the most functional
direction. Law as a means of protecting the individual against the
social system, as a basis for the support of human rights, is less developed than law as a means for society to impress its will upon
the individual.

But to return for a further word on the question of moral issues. There have been many changes in the penal systems of
technically advanced countries in recent years. It is very doubtful,
however, that any of these changes have resulted from the impact
of hard scientific evidence obtained through rigorous research
methods. The humanities rather than science must be credited
with what changes there have been. Nothing is said against this, except that there are other considerations which can be taken into
account. The Anglo-Saxon Protestant ethic has had a considerable impact upon the penal systems of many countries, in the East as
well as the West. But an ethic is not a technology. Ways for solving
problems are very similar in all cultures, and ethics has nothing to

say about what is a rigorous deduction. However, the types of solutions arrived at may be suitable to one social ethic and not to another. A positive result in one culture may become a negative result in another culture. The *ways* in which problems may be solved may be exportable, but not so the solutions derived, by whatever means. Further, two solutions that may independently be effective or good may, when compounded, become ineffective or even bad (that is, have an effect opposite to that desired). In other words, two good things, when added together, do not necessarily become better than either singly.

Many criminologists claim that criminology is a science. The relationship between science and ethics is another point of debate, although in this particular case some simplification is possible by replacing the term "science" with "scientific method." The scientific method is not directly concerned with values because with values, questions of proof do not arise. The information generated regarding a particular area and comprising a field of knowledge, also often termed "science," impinges more upon consideration of values than does the method whereby the information is derived. Knowledge of ways in which solutions to problems may be sought (method) is different from knowledge of solutions to problems as they are obtained. A knowledge of factor analysis—the means whereby "general intelligence" was "discovered"—is quite different from knowledge of the intelligence test scores of persons derived from the application of this method. It may, of course, be quite valid to challenge the solution to a problem by reference to the means used in obtaining it, but the demonstration that the means was inappropriate in a particular case does not suggest that it (that is, the method) lacks validity in other applications. Statistical counts of the numbers of persons received into prisons may be quite accurate as such, but such counts are not measures of the amount of crime. The method of counting may be quite unexceptional, but it is much more difficult to discuss the utility or meaning of such counts for any practical purposes other than prison provisioning, determination of budget requirements for escort personnel, vehicles for conveyance of the committed persons, and similar uses.

With these points in mind, we will stress not what is known, but what is unknown. We have particularly tried to deal with the ways in which things may become known. When we criticize earlier work, we do not intend to reflect adversely upon the persons who, in accord with scientific practice, are named. There are others whose work is based on similar fallacies who are not quoted, and hence, not named. The writer has also been heavily critical of some of his own earlier work. If there were no need to be critical, knowledge would remain static. Fortunately, this is not the case.

The negative aspects of this work will quickly become apparent to the reader. Those who may feel discouraged by this might first read Chapter 10. There are certain things that are known in this field, and there are many more things that are not yet known. The emphasis on the latter is intended to be a challenge to all, and indeed, especially, to the author himself.

1

Facts and figures

"Facts and figures," although often taken together as a phrase, are not necessarily similar. Whether a figure is or is not a fact is often a difficult question, even without any attempt to delve into the semantics or philosophy involved in the concept of fact. Various statistics produced by governmental and other agencies purport to throw light upon problems of crime. However, few figures are available that may be claimed to relate either directly or indirectly to our subject. We can find out how many persons are in prison or similar institutions on any day in any country or other defined area, but whether they are being "effectively treated" is a different matter altogether.

Perhaps one measure of the treatment of offenders or the effectiveness of punishment (these two concepts will be treated as a representation of a combined operation for the moment) is the rate of "recidivism." Recidivism usually means the frequency of return to crime after some form of disposal by the courts. Almost as many definitions of recidivism exist as there are jurisdictions.

Some jurisdictions define recidivists as those who are returned to prison, ignoring those who may subsequently commit an offense and be committed to a local jail for a period of as long as one year; other jurisdictions regard any further offense as warranting the classification of recidivist, although in most cases certain subsequent minor crimes are excluded. Different jurisdictions draw different distinctions between minor offenses and major offenses. For example, in the United States the term "crime" includes both felonies and misdemeanors, whereas in England and Wales the term "crime" means an offense for which the offender *could be* tried on indictment (that is, an indictable offense or a hybrid). Again, in England and Wales the criminal statistics that report recidivism relate to "offenders returned to prison" (16, Appendix 10, official prison statistics). In the United States it is possible for a person to be termed a recidivist without having a new crime proved against him, if, because of failure to maintain parole conditions, he is reincarcerated. In general, however, the term "technical violator" seems to be preferred for the parole violator. The consequences of being termed a "recidivist" also vary according to the law of different states, but in most of the United States an offender who is designated recidivist is denied probation and is liable to more serious punishments. In England and Wales, however, there are no such limitations on the uses of probation, nor are there restrictions regarding the imposition of a minimum-length sentence (16). Even within the continental United States the possession of burglary tools is a felony in about half the states and a misdemeanor in the other half.

No matter what definition is regarded as more satisfactory, some measurement associated with a relapse into "criminal ways" (whatever that might mean) is clearly related to the concept of the effectiveness of the system of punishment-treatment. There is a vague similarity between all the general measurements proposed. Let us accept as a basis for our initial discussion this vague similarity as a sufficient frame of reference from which to begin.

RECIDIVISM

In matters that relate to recidivism there appear to be many figures but very few facts. In order to throw light upon the problem of the effectiveness of punishment-treatment, it is necessary to dis-

tinguish carefully between facts and figures and to consider the
nature of data that may serve as a foundation for valid inferences.
Many have found that figures which are claimed to give information about reconvictions after treatment (recidivism) generally fail
to meet critical tests or even to withstand careful examination (see
pages 52–53). The main difficulty does not arise from uncertainties with respect to the methods by which persons or events
are counted, but rather it arises from the descriptions of the persons and the definitions of the events which are not relevant to the
operational questions being asked. Another problem arises from
the lack of training in sampling and other statistical techniques of
most persons who claim to do research in the criminological field.
Serious errors are to be found in almost every study that has used
a sampling method, and nearly all studies must utilize sampling,
whether the sample is 100 percent at a point in time or some
smaller fraction for a period of time. Whether a 100 percent sample is a "sample" or not, depends upon the nature of the inference,
rather than the method of the selection of cases used as a basis for
the study. The majority of the kinds of errors detected in both recent and earlier work are sufficiently serious to render both the
positive and negative findings suspect. This is a sweeping charge,
and we will state evidence in some detail so that the reader may
judge for himself.

■ *Comparative rates and experiences*

In countries where there are no statutory limitations on the award of
probation by the courts, it has been shown that the rate of recidivism
for those placed on probation is about one in five, while for those
who are given some form of institutional treatment the rate is
around one in every two. These figures are quoted to give an indication of the order of difference between the two forms of treatment
where the court has considerable discretion. Do these figures mean
that probation is better than punishment? It would even be possible
to find claims of this kind in respectable publications. Clearly the
rate of recidivism is a function of the selection for probation. Since
first offenders are so-called good risks, no matter what form of disposal the court may use, and probation is more often considered
appropriate for first offenders than for others, even where there
are no restrictions upon its use, the total sum of the risks in a probation caseload will be less than the sum of the risk in other sys-

tems of treatment. Only if the courts were acting as randomizing agents would there be an expected similarity between the rates for different treatments (71). In general we may say that the nature of the "input" to a system is one of the variables to be considered in discussing the "output." The gross comparisons between probation and other forms of treatment, indeed any other forms of gross statistical comparisons, are, at the very least, misleading. The further deduction that is also often claimed from gross comparisons between probation and incarceration, that the superior results of probation indicate that probation is superior to punishment as a form of treatment, is also invalid, even if it were possible to standardize for the "input" differences. Prison may include some elements of treatment, and probation may include some elements of punishment. No assumptions regarding the effectiveness of punishment as distinct from treatment can be supported by existing evidence, since it seems best to assume that all forms of disposal for offenders contain a mixture of both concepts.

The mixture of punishment and treatment raises some extremely complex problems. Even the concept of punishment is unsatisfactory as a unitary concept in considering human reaction. Only in simple conditioning situations with animals may assumptions regarding reward and punishment be made without the probability of a very serious error in oversimplification. The zero point (base for reference) between reward and punishment may be assumed for animals, and even the validity of this assumption may be open to challenge. However, with humans, the zero point is not determined by "objective" states, but rather by a level of expectation derived from a body of experience or history. A person who has experienced living at the rate of $100,000 a year for many years would find living at the rate of $10,000 a year "punishment," whereas a person conditioned to living at a rate of $7,000 a year might well find $10,000 a year rewarding, other things being equal (72, p. 76). To some extent, it may be safe to generalize that, for normal persons, physical punishment, incarceration, or even restrictions imposed by probation are considered forms of punishment, since each places undesired limitations upon the individual's behavior. Nonetheless, it is also true that one person cannot determine what is severe or light punishment for any other person. It has even been shown that imprisonment can be "rewarding" for some persons, in that it conveys status upon them with regard to their peer group.

GENERAL SOCIAL CONTROLS
(GENERAL PREVENTION)

Attention has become focused on the effects of treatments or punishments on persons subjected to them. But it must be accepted that if offenders were subjected to no forms of control, this would have an influence upon society as a whole. Perhaps the criminal, or at least what happens to him, provides some positive function for society. The criminal affords a symbol of the sacrificial offering, acting as a means for the integration of the larger society and supporting the values it desires to maintain.

The law as a means for enforcement of morals has been debated with respect to general philosophical considerations and with regard to specific acts. The discussions usually focus upon some aspect of "crimes without victims," such as homosexuality and prostitution. The only reason to mention this topic here is to note that forms of treatment to which offenders may be subjected is a different matter from information about that form of treatment as a means for deterring others from engaging in the activity thus "treated." A form of treatment that might best reform the offender might not be the same as one that would best deter others. For example, as someone remarked, sentencing a homosexual to a prison is rather like sentencing a drunkard to a brewery! An all-male society (prison) might seem attractive to a confirmed homosexual!

■ *Justice seen to be done?*

It should also be noted that if the public at large were not to become aware of what was done to offenders and were not to perceive these actions as a direct result of offenses, there would be no reason to suppose that behavior would be modified in any way because of such action. Thus it is not what is in fact done to the offender, but information about what is done that may influence the general public, and hence act as a social control. There is another important distinction here. Much of what is done to offenders is not reported widely; hence, it cannot have any influence upon others, because it is unknown to them. Ignorance may be some form of social control, but it differs from information in its process and function. Perhaps people are deterred from committing crimes more by what they believe to be the likely consequences than by what would actually be likely to happen to them. Beliefs may not be very closely related to facts. As W. I. Thomas remarked: "Situations which are defined as real are real in their consequences" (62). This problem, although an extremely interesting and important one, is not touched upon in the body of this work. However, because prevention is a factor that cannot be completely ignored in discussion of treatment and punishment, some further notes are given as Appendix A (pages 157–162).

It should be apparent that figures do not exist relating to the impact of the sentencing policy of different jurisdictions upon members of the general public. Inferences from large-scale trends over time in the "crime rate" do not provide a basis for assessment of this factor. [See "New Thinking in Criminal Statistics" (73).] Like the dark figures of undetected and unreported crime, the information regarding the general-prevention effects of penal policies remain unknown but very significant dimensions. Even the use of the term "treatment" rather than punishment to describe what is done to offenders upon conviction puts the doctrines of deterrence in a different perspective. Punishment might be seen as a deterrent not only to the person punished, but also to others who have not committed crimes, by reason of the example it affords. Treatment, on the other hand, does not necessarily connote punishment or even shame. The idea of vicarious learning is also involved. Certainly to do something to the individual who needs treatment, not because it will have any effect upon him but because it may have an influence on others who have not been involved as yet with similar acts, cannot by definition be treatment.

THE PROBLEM—A SUMMARY STATEMENT

■ *What is punishment or treatment?*

Assessments of treatment of offenders are concerned with a large number of variables for which data often do not exist. If punishment as a concept is concerned with the dual evaluation of penal systems in terms of "punishment-treatment," the problem becomes even greater. Perhaps punishment may be defined as what is done to the offender as a person with the partial purpose of influencing others (the general-prevention aspect of the system), while what is done to him as an individual with a view to reducing his probability of committing further offenses may be termed treatment. This does not, of course, mean that the nonoffending public will view all qualities of the treatment as lacking elements of punishment in one and the same event. Alternatively, if it is discovered as a *matter of fact* that a particular operation which may be subjectively classified as "punishment" results in reducing the probability that an offender will commit further crimes, then this particular operation is "treatment." Thus, we may operationally define "treatment" as that which tends to reduce the probability of recidivism (recurrence of the crime or symptom of the illness which gave rise to the criminal act). However, the death penalty is a most positive way of preventing further crimes by the offender concerned, but it would not be appropriate to refer to this operation as "treatment"; it is presumably punishment, although many murderers often seek their own self-destruction after committing the crime and some do not succeed. Is helping them to succeed in what they failed to do for themselves punishment or treatment? It seems difficult to arrive at a satisfactory definition of "treatment of offenders" by this means of argument. It may be suggested that everything else which is done today for and to offenders, other than the death penalty, is "treatment." Indeed, such an assumption seems to fit the language used by those concerned in the correctional systems of the advanced countries.

It must be admitted that not all of the things which go on in prisons and other institutions are "treatment," as some of these operations are "housekeeping functions" necessary to maintain the institution and to ensure the security of the offender. It is generally claimed that it is difficult to say when the "housekeeping functions" cease and "treatment" begins, because an offender may be influenced toward a better life by various personal contacts, including those not defined or even perceived as "treatment-oriented." It seems necessary, therefore, to retain some statement in the definition of treatment that relates to the increased probability of desirable outcome associated with the operation thus defined. But even this approach has some unsatisfactory elements.

Electroconvulsive therapy is usually regarded as "treatment" for certain mental disorders. To an observer this treatment seems to be a painful process. Indeed, if one were not given the situation and its intent, it would be very difficult to distinguish this "treatment" from punishment or even torture. Mere observation of the situation itself does not contain the information that enables the observer to say that it is "treatment." This may be a rather dramatic and unusual example, but it must be admitted that many medicines are unpleasant to take, yet there is no doubt about the proper application of the term "treatment" to their use.

The distinction between treatment and punishment may be better appreciated if it is noted that one of the major characteristics of treatment is that it is directly and perhaps only related to beliefs about the well-being of *the person treated*. The death penalty is clearly not acceptable as beneficial to the person subjected to it; hence, it may be consistently excluded from the concept of "treatment" by this form of argument. It might be suggested, at least tentatively, that treatment becomes punishment (no matter what is done) when there is any element of consideration for persons other than the person "treated," no matter how minute these considerations may be. Whenever there is a consideration that by doing something to Mr. X (the offender or patient) some other person or persons (society or those in authority) will benefit in some way, then that something, whatever else it might be, is not treatment. It may be punishment or something that is neither punishment nor treatment, but it clearly cannot be classified as "treatment." This would even apply to those operations which serve merely to establish or enhance the pay or status of those who carry out the operations.

This definition is still unsatisfactory because it helps only by excluding certain operations, by saying what treatment is not rather than what it is. Accordingly it is necessary to retain the concept of outcome for the person who is the subject of the operations, excluding those covered by external references as others. We may say that treatment consists of those operations which are intended to benefit the offender through the reduction of the probability that he will offend again and can be shown to have such an effect. In other words, until it can be established that the operation concerned has the consequence of reducing the probability of recidivism, this operation should not be classified as treatment, and we may not know what it is. It may be punishment. It may be something that those who carry out the operations have persuaded the public to let them do to persons defined as criminals which may serve mainly to provide a professional structure for themselves. What is done may or may not be functional for society as a whole.

Definitions are difficult enough. Operational definitions that rely upon evidence of the outcome of operations are much more difficult because the problems are complex, and there is insufficient information upon which to base assessments that can command confidence.

■ *The complex issues involved*

There are so many variables or factors that must be considered in relation to any assessment of what is done to and for offenders that it is possible only to indicate an approximate degree of complexity. The nature of the complexity of the treatment-punishment function may be illustrated by the number of variables identified in the following statement:

Persons who vary in ways that are in the main unknown (variable X_1), live in situations (X_2), and are exposed to cultural influences that vary in unknown ways (X_3). They sometimes commit deeds (X_4) which vary in many ways, except that they are classified by the laws of society as crimes, and these laws (X_5) also vary both in content and interpretation. Some persons are detected by systems that vary in unspecified ways (X_6); these are dealt with by persons or courts that also vary in their policies (X_7) and are allocated to institutions (X_8) that also differ from each other in many unknown ways. They are committed for varying periods of time (X_9), and their interaction with the treatment (X_{10}) is expected to vary. In most cases they may be expected to interact with other persons (X_{11}) also undergoing treatment. Eventually, they are released to situations that vary both in themselves and in terms of the expected interaction with the personality of the former inmate (X_{12}). In consideration of recidivism, this process may be seen as repeated many times. Frequently in discussions of recidivism the number of times the circuit has been completed remains unspecified.

Thus, "treatment" in institutions or in other settings is a small subsystem that is involved with other subsystems and embedded within a much larger system. The largest system to which we will refer here is our concept of "society." Is this situation too complex to be subjected to analysis by scientific methods? Should we stop trying to be rigorous and rely upon subjective judgments and feelings of the situation? Can research designs take into account all of these variables? Can subjective judgment cope with the complexity any better? By using the more rigorous forms of analysis, it is possible to take complexity into account, while fully appreciating the limitations of such a method. That this is true is indicated by the fact that the very involved descriptions of variables, above, can be reduced to a simple system diagram. Through application of the scientific method we can best reduce the complex syntax of our problems into manageable form; through the use of such methods, the human mind attempts to cope with the difficulties inherent in the nature of the problem itself.

It is sometimes argued that resorting to "facts and figures" obscures the essentially human considerations in any decisions that may be taken in this and related fields of human endeavor. There is no evidence that human intuition is any more effective in arriving at socially desirable solutions than the "facts and figures" approach. Neither can claim much success to date. The human intuitive approach has been tried for many centuries, while the attempt to use more rigorous and controlled approaches based on systems analysis is only beginning. The selection of a method for solving problems cannot be decided rationally in terms of any attributes of the methods themselves; rather, we should utilize the method which achieves the socially desired outcomes with precision and possibly least cost. A relationship does exist between a rational strategy for selection of methods to attack problems and the strategy applied to solve the problem itself, but the relationship is not a simple one. We shall return to this concept after discussion of the present state of knowledge in the particular area of punishment-treatment.

Uncertainty and the unique person

In dealing with offenders we are dealing with persons, and we must not lose sight of this fact, regardless of what scientific methods or systems are used to assist in the making of decisions. This is much the same as saying that moral values cannot be suspended in running institutions, for the sake of efficiency or operational tidiness. It does not follow that the subjective assessment of personality features believed to be unique to the individual who is under discussion or treatment is either a more moral or a more efficient way of handling such items of information. The emphasis upon the uniqueness of the personality is usually put forward as an argument for the rejection of any *impersonal* methods of data analysis concerning the individual. What are regarded as "impersonal methods" vary according to the personal uniqueness of the critic, but generally include the use of any forms of mathematical analysis and often also methods of logical analysis expressed in a symbolic form. Linguistic forms in terms of plain language are more generally acceptable. In operational terms, the objection may normally be reduced to the use of any symbols other than ordinary language or the language of the particular discipline in which the critic has been schooled.

While the uniqueness of the individual offender must be accepted, so too is the person assessing the offender and making decisions about him. These two unique patterns of personality do not provide a better basis for moral or rational action than that which may be provided by other means in relation to other concepts of personality and the decision process. The factor of uniqueness has nothing to do with either morals or efficiency; uniqueness is not a feature only of man. Unique, once-and-for-all events occur in many sectors of the universe as man experiences and describes it. The claim to uniqueness is not the same as a claim to humanity (whatever that may mean), though critics often confound the two.

No once-and-for-all or unique event is of any value for the provision of guidance for the future while it is perceived in that form. If, by definition, the same thing cannot happen twice, then there is nothing to be gained by our experience of it the first (and only) time. If, however, we do find similarities, we may begin to utilize classifications based on these similarities and hence utilize our experience. But this means that the event is no longer seen as unique. Rather, the situation is seen as having some characteristics which might be unique and some which are supposed not to be unique, or the uniqueness is seen as being constituted by the unique patterning of items which are not unique in themselves; that is, it is the arrangement which is unique, not the things, events, characteristics, or anything else. But again, if it is postulated that the items are not unique, then neither is the patterning. For general purposes it may be reasonable to regard the patterning as unique because the number of possible arrangements for the nonunique items may be so great. But the claim to being able to describe a great variety of patterns is not the same as the claim to being able to describe uniqueness, no matter how many possible varieties of arrangements there are.

Fingerprints are commonly considered to be unique, at least as unique as the individual person. However, even if fingerprints were accepted as unique, it would be a useless fact. The uniqueness of the fingerprint cannot be put to any use; usefulness lies in the similarity between the prints found in different locations, such as one in a police file and the other at the scene of a crime.

VARIETY AND CLASSIFICATION

The similarities between unique fingerprints provide the sole basis for inference. In fact, fingerprints (as classified) are not as unique as most laymen believe (36, p. 70). The variety in the system of fingerprint classification must, however, be sufficiently great to permit many millions of prints to be classified under different patterns of identification. But a further assumption in the use of fingerprints is that the patterns lack the propensity to change with time. Thus, fingerprints can be used, or, more correctly, classifications of fingerprint impressions can be used, because similarities may be noted and because we may assume considerable *invariance* between any two impressions at different times. It is also assumed that the classification of a print is unlikely to vary between persons who may take the print; the print taker in any particular case is sufficiently similar in all operationally necessary respects to any other person who might have taken the print. The same assumptions apply to classifications of prints.

The form of analysis we have used to discuss the operational utility of fingerprints and the nature of legitimate inference that may be drawn from classifications of print impressions may be generalized to all characteristics of persons. The fact that the fingerprint is a physical feature while other features we may wish to describe are psychological or emotional is insignificant in this particular regard.

When we accept the individual's uniqueness, we may question whether the nature of uniqueness may differ among various characteristics with which we are concerned in respect to the treatment of offenders. Fingerprints may serve well for purposes of identification, and the arguments put forward may be conceded for this purpose, but for purposes of assessing forms of treatment, a different uniqueness applies. If the complex patterning of nonunique features gives rise to a large variety of possible types it may be convenient to regard each of these as unique, and this is one form of uniqueness. But it may be claimed that there are characteristics which are unique to individuals and not merely complex arrangements of characteristics common to other persons.

Such argument is totally unsound. Insofar as it is possible to discuss or explain individual behavior, personality, or indeed any feature of any one person, we are restricted to concepts of combinations of attributes that have been recognized elsewhere and in other persons. If any unique characteristic were to exist in any person, how would any other person recognize it? If it were possible to recognize it, it would not be possible to describe it because there would be no semantic convention (word) by which this characteristic could be denoted except perhaps in the private language of the individual describer. If any person resorts to a language which only he can claim to understand, he is most likely to be classified as schizophrenic and his much prized personal language classified as babbling.

INFORMATION IN RELATION TO UNIQUENESS

Thus, we must come to terms with the fact that in all practical situations we have to make decisions as though the persons involved were not unique, while at the same time we must accept the doctrine that all persons are unique.

How does this come about? Is there a more rational means of expressing this dilemma? There is, if we are prepared to accept certain concepts that do not find ready acceptance in the minds of those who oppose the application of scientific methods to the attempted solution of human problems.

Decisions relate to information; information reduces uncertainty; uncertainty will never be eliminated; the uniqueness of the individual is another way of expressing the previous statement. Furthermore, we are concerned with making decisions under conditions of uncertainty.

Those who would claim to be certain are rejecting the concept of the uniqueness of the individual, while loudly claiming that they are the ones who can recognize it. The claim to recognize the uniqueness of an individual is usually made along with the suggestion that this uniqueness may also be uniquely understood by the claimant. Such claims to understanding usually take refuge in a simplistic formulation of a wide philosophy ("It's all so simple really!"), and because it is so simple to the claimant, he is also extremely self-assured regarding his claimed understanding. This development leads to rejection of the scientific method which accepts uncertainty as basic to knowledge, with the rejection of all other

views which are not in accord with the particular personally preferred simplistic formulation.

If the claimant does not have much power over others, his simple
certainty will not do much harm, because, for each certainty he
holds, others will hold other and different certainties. If he were to
become a dictator, it would be better for the majority of the people
if he could develop some appreciation for the scientific method and
its humility in the face of complexity and even uniqueness: in a
word, its accommodation of uncertainty.

ACTION UNDER CONDITIONS
OF UNCERTAINTY

Uncertainty may seem disabling. Perhaps that is why there is so
much searching for panaceas, for a prepackaged philosophy or an
instant cure. How is the feeling of inadequacy that most people
feel when they say "I don't know," to be reconciled with the scientist's searching activity? If one really must say that one does not
know the answer to a problem, how can one make a reasonable decision? Such problems have received considerable attention in recent years, particularly in regard to modern techniques of warfare.

Operational research techniques developed mainly during World
War II have been adapted and adopted in many fields of manage-
ment and a large body of decision theory has emerged. We will consider the details of such developments as they relate to the evaluation of penal-treatment processes after we have examined some
examples of research that indicate the nature of the approach.

Problems of classification and uniqueness based on the concept
of the complexity of attribute constellations within individuals are
not fundamentally different from those that may be derived from
the theory of measurement. If we could measure only one thing
with absolute accuracy, whatever that thing might be, we might
expect to arrive at the concept of uniqueness. If, for example, we
could measure every person's height or weight with absolute accuracy (or with very great accuracy) on any day, every person would
be found to be of a different height or weight. If we measured height
or weight approximately, we would find many persons who were
"alike" in that they had the same height or weight. Uniqueness is a
feature of the extent to which we can separate small differences.
But in all practical situations we do not utilize the fact that every-

body is of a different height or weight, that is, unique on these measurement scales. For example, we know that persons who are grossly overweight have a shorter life expectation, but we cannot state a specific value or a critical point at which a person becomes overweight. We could not utilize the important association between weight and the expectation of life if we insisted that every person at any particular time was of a unique weight. Only when we are prepared to make inaccurate statements do these statements have any utility. This applies whether we are using a subjective assessment based on our accumulated and internalized experience or the scientific method.

We use measurements of height, weight, or other factors that are sufficiently accurate for the particular purposes we have in mind. Measurement for its own sake has no utility, and an external factor or purpose must be invoked. For example, the value of pi (π) is an infinite series. In one sense we can say that the true value is unknown, but we do not argue against using the various approximate values of π that are available (e.g., 3.1415), and we select the value according to the purpose we have in mind. To illustrate a general point, the use of π is related to the accuracy with which we can make other measurements. There is no means to assess the value of information in terms of anything within itself but only with reference to some kind of external criteria.

It may then be claimed that measurement is always approximate and that the number and degree of accuracy of the measurements we may seek can be evaluated only with respect to a specific purpose. It is not sufficient to indicate that certain qualities have not been measured accurately or even that certain qualities have not been taken into consideration in a research inquiry, without also showing that omitted measurements or the inaccuracy of the assessments were of significance in relation to the purposes of the study. This kind of reasoning applies whatever the basis for the inferences drawn from evidence of whatever kind.

3

Problems of inference in research into penal treatment

The best research in the fields of criminology and penology seldom seem to do more than clarify the unknown. It is doubtful whether even the most enthusiastic research worker in these fields could sustain a claim to having added significantly to knowledge. Myths and beliefs of the past have little or no support when subjected to rigorous examination, but in their place only the most tentative suggestions can be brought forward. This is perhaps to be expected and is hardly to be regretted. More regretable is the fact that all too often research ends by noting nothing more significant than that the questions with which the project began were inappropriate. But these types of research are, in the main, the more satisfactory studies. Most research projects make larger or more "practical" claims and usually lack validity when subjected to critical assessment.

THE IMPROPER QUESTIONS

There are two basic reasons as to why this is so. First and perhaps
the more important is the fact that most research studies have attempted too much, and the available resources of ideas and personnel have been spread too thinly over too diverse an area (see,
for example, pages 33 & 80). The second reason may be that researchers in this field have scavenged techniques from far and wide
in the social and other sciences without due regard to the limitations
implied in the borrowed methods. Techniques that may suffice to
satisfy intellectual curiosity with regard to tenable theories in one
field of inquiry may appear attractive in another. Some techniques have proved so attractive that the questions which they can
answer have been assumed to be relevant to the field of criminology when in fact they are not. Sometimes the answers have been
no more than semiattached to the questions, and at other times the
questions have been tailored to suit the means for finding "answers."

Thus, the first reason in the preceding paragraph suggests a partial explanation of some of the weaknesses of these researches in
that the questions have been inappropriate to the techniques available, while the second reason suggests that the research questions
when modified to fit the techniques have not been satisfactory questions. In other words, we have managed to get either the questions
or the means to answer them right, but we have not achieved a
satisfactory matching of techniques to meaningful questions. Problems of two distinct kinds are thus involved in the necessary match
of questions with techniques to investigate them.

Most questions asked about crimes, prisoners, prisons, treatment,
and punishment are phrased in the language of rhetoric (see, for
example, pages 46–47). Not only are value concepts involved, but
many more elements are included that make the translation into
scientific questions difficult. It may be noted in passing that some
drama, novels, and all forms of mass-media entertainment continue
to utilize crime as one of their major topics. Yet in attempting to deal
with crime and offenders we are concerned not with the dramatic
incident but with a mass phenomenon. There is a large gap between
the two kinds of information regarding crime that the public is
provided: (1) news headlines and stories of particular criminal in-

cidents, and (2) statistical counts (such as numbers of crimes known to the police or persons proceeded against).

Usually only one crime in several hundred will have those qualities which make it seem valuable as a "story" and hence worth printing as news or noting in other media. For purposes of illustration only, suppose that one such case in every hundred is rated as "newsworthy." This may be far too large a proportion, but accepting this as a tentative figure, then between the one reported and the one hundred recorded only statistically there are ninety-nine others, few perhaps with any marked similarities to those headlined and discussed.

It seems fair to assume that the basis of information upon which most persons can frame their questions is unsatisfactory. Yet, the democratic process is the basis for law; hence, it is also the basis for classifying persons as criminals and the consequences which follow from that. It is, therefore, neither possible nor desirable to dismiss all laymen's questions as irrrelevant to scientific inquiry. It becomes essential to attempt the difficult process of translating the questions that were posed initially in an unsuitable language.

It is necessary to isolate problems where the questions that may be asked are highly specific and subject to rigorous analysis. But these questions must be meaningful in terms similar to the original question. If it is necessary to translate the question into a different language from the original in order to facilitate an attack upon the problem thus phrased, then the answers must be retranslated into the form of language in which the untransformed question was put. It is unsatisfactory to conclude that answers to the questions raised by the public cannot be found, and it is equally unsatisfactory for those of us who are professionally concerned to seek instead to answer questions arising out of our own professionalism.

MISAPPLIED STATISTICS

Many research workers have revealed a preoccupation with the idea of statistical *significance*. Their work is characterized by the use or misuse of *chi-squared,* the *T-test,* and other measures of *significance*. But this *significance* relates only to the probability of the results arising from chance factors. Whether a result is *significant* or not in this meaning of the term is frequently only a matter of the size of the sample studied or even of the number of possible items that could reach a given level of probability. The greater the number of independent tests used on any sample, the greater the probability that some will be *significant* by chance. Workers in this area seldom understand or appreciate the difference between *significance* and *estimation*. It may be taken as a general rule of thumb that in penology *significance* is of *no* significance, but *estimation* may provide a more realistic means of assessing the power of the results of an inquiry.

For many projects the preceding comments are already at far too sophisticated a level. Even the basic distinction between setting up and testing hypotheses is often not appreciated. Still less frequently are the research strategies employed or designed to maximize one or the other of these distinct types of operation. Indeed it is the rule rather than the exception that sample sizes are too large merely to serve the purposes of hypothesis hunting in an economic manner, and at the same time they are too small to test prior assumptions except in the crudest possible fashion.

In some types of inquiry the demonstration that the hypothesis can be sustained rather than rejected may be an adequate criteria of increased knowledge in the field. In criminology and, perhaps, even more extensively in the field of social research, the rejection or otherwise of the null hypothesis is not the end, but only possibly a valid *beginning*. Yet few researches report further.

THE SO-WHAT QUESTION

In any well-designed research, before any work other than the initial thinking has been completed, the research worker should be able to specify the nature and types of possible outcomes—if only as a fundamental probability set. For example, if he proposes to examine four hypotheses, H_1 may or may not be rejected, H_2 may or may not be rejected, and so on; the pattern of outcomes can be indicated as possible configurations of unknowns that will either become knowns or else uncertainty will be confirmed at the conclusion of the study. This information should be used to further modify the design by reference to the question: If all hypotheses are sustained, in pattern A, then what?; alternatively, if pattern B, then what?; and so on for all possible outcome patterns available from the design. The answers to the "then what" questions under the different probable conditions *after the experiment* provide a means for assessing the power of the initial design, that is, *before the experiment is put into effect*.

Because it is possible, albeit with uncertainty, to visualize the necessity of having to make further moves in relation to any research design, the contingencies are sufficiently real to need consideration. Alternative research designs can be evaluated by reference to the different types of answers to the "then what" types of questions that may be generated in the initial stages. The fact is that after many research studies are completed and reported upon, it is still not possible to get a very meaningful answer to "then what" (or even "so what") questions. This seems to indicate that when satisfactory answers cannot be supplied at the initial stages, there is a prima facie case to suspect that it might be better to replace the proposed design.

Is there then a serious malaise afflicting research in criminology? Why is so much attempted and so little achieved? Are the claims justified that criminological research is in a perilous state? There is now wide agreement among research critics in the field that all is not well, but relatively large sums of money are being invested in research. Is it then justified to claim that most of this money is being wasted? And if so, who is to blame? Or, perhaps more important, what can be done?

Crime, as we have noted, is always in the public eye. The amount of material the citizen reads about crime leads him to believe that more than enough is already known, and he clamors for action. And, echoing this, the authorities must decide to do something rather than to find out anything. Those who provide funds are very close to the pressure for action. Thus, there is a tendency to support more of the same kinds of action, rather then to challenge that which is being done by theoretical development. After all, the authorities cannot admit that what is being done is not correct; it might be insufficient, and more is needed of the "good things" that are already being practiced.

Projects known by the term "action-research" have recently become popular. In a large proportion of these cases, however, the second side of the hyphen means little more than the label on the bottle of a popular medicament! Some aspects of the "action" are doubtless new and represent imaginative approaches to some problems, but there is no way of knowing which components of the total program will prove useful and which wasteful, because of the way the whole thing is packaged. For an example of an action program with both useful and wasteful components, see *Social Policy* (72). Problems need specific boundary conditions before they can be set or solved. We can move forward only if we are content to move step by step, and only if we can be sure that at each step we are on firm ground before attempting to take another. Great leaps forward are rare in all spheres of life, and when they do occur it is because of an admixture of good luck and the fact that somebody who could recognize the propitious situation was ready to catch and secure it. Good luck is something we should be ready to capitalize upon when it arises, but we cannot plan for it nor bank on its coming our way. Most valuable research is the result of hard work, not the result of a cat (black or otherwise) knocking over a laboratory milk bottle or a similar coincidence. Some discoveries have been *made* in these kinds of ways, but they were never *planned* in these kinds of ways—if they had been, they could not have succeeded. We are, as it were, trying to find stepping stones through the slough of our ignorance, and we cannot take any "great leap forward" from an insecure foothold.

If we knew even less than we do, but knew it more certainly, we might be in a better position, but in criminology a certain amount is known with great uncertainty. Our present task is to communicate this uncertainty.

TYPES OF LANGUAGE

With regard to types of language, we are likely to meet difficulties arising from the situation noted earlier, the proximity of criminology to ethics. Uncertainty is not well received in the areas of morals and beliefs. Criminals have "done wrong," and a value system that implicitly relies upon absolutes is invoked. Values are not normally perceived as variables. The language of the scientific method and the language of belief systems utilize a different grammar. We will briefly examine some of the semantic problems.

■ *The problem of languages*

Words come to have meaning by convention to those who use them, excluding cases of definition that are achieved by redundancy. Communication is often inhibited because both the scientist and the layman use words that are spelled the same but in use and conotation have different meanings. Consider in this regard the term "intelligence." If the scientist is to share his information with the layman and with other scientists in different fields, then a process of two-way communication must be established. Regardless how wise a person may be or how much he knows, his knowledge is of no value, and indeed there is no way of knowing whether it *is* knowledge unless and until it is communciated.

The concept of social pathology relies in part upon the concept of society. Society, for the most part, consists of laymen, and it is to be hoped that nobody regrets this! Meaningful research concerning crime and other social ills must find ways to accommodate the juxtaposition of the scientific method and moral or value concepts. This would seem to require that a means be found to relate the language of science to the language of belief systems and morals. This presents many difficulties, and it would be easy to get involved in tortuous and heavy philosophical discussion. We will only note a few points in this regard, and even these must be treated somewhat superficially here. Nonetheless, some indication of the communication problem is necessary to establish some background for later critical analysis of the status of knowledge in penal and criminological research.

The efficiency of words may be assessed with respect to two criteria, each related to the purpose it is intended should be served:

1. How well words convey meaning, and whether they are effective for communication
2. How useful words are for manipulation of concepts by the processes of logic, and whether they assist rational thinking

A system of communication that had all of the first and none of the second would be deficient over-all.

The jargon that grows up around any area of specialization provides an indication that normal language has been found to be deficient in either the first or second criterion. In the social sciences it is usually the first that generated the jargon, whereas in mathematics the second (relating to operators and operations) generated special terms. The development of symbolic logic is an indication that "ordinary language" has been found deficient in the second criterion and inadequate for processes of reasoning. To be effective, communication requires redundancy, whereas redundancy is a handicap in logical manipulations.

It must be agreed that there is no difference in principle between the use of words which, after all, are only symbols and the use of abstract symbols that may be translated into words. The difference in approach between mathematical or symbolic logic and the layman's use of ordinary language lies wholly or mainly in the fact that most people have a reasonable facility with ordinary language, whereas fewer have been trained in the language of mathematics or related disciplines. Most persons thus seek to use the same system of ordinary language for both communication and for reasoning and logical analysis—for both the first and second criteria. But the rational choice would be to choose the system most suited to the particular purpose. Thus, when we wish to communicate with a maximum number of persons, we would use the plainest and most ordinary language; when we have a highly complex set of concepts to manipulate, we would be advised to avoid the complexity introduced by redundancy and select as our medium a "2" type language system. There is a world of difference between a poem and an equation; we cannot say that we prefer one to the other just because it *is* a poem or an equation.

Communication is a central concept in much social casework and penal treatment. The verbal therapies are well established and take many forms. Some therapists study the detail of oral exchanges (transactions) and interpret behavioral problems by reference to the patterns they deduce. Such theories of communication in therapeutic situations assume that the language in which the transactions are expressed conveys emotional content as well as information. The messages are highly-coded expressions of feelings. In this sense transaction theory treats language like a poem, with much highly-coded information that is designed to appeal to emotion rather than to reason. This may be a valid way to consider some forms of communication, but the transaction-analysis method could not be applied to an equation nor to much legal, scientific, or any other types of the second-language category. However, the facility that social workers develop for examining language in its highly coded forms provides a framework with which they may tend to consider other forms of language and other forms of problems. On the other hand, the social scientist is more familiar with language for the purpose of communicating information rather than feeling and for the manipulation of concepts.

The social scientist and the social caseworker often have difficulty in communicating with each other, not because they do not understand what is said but because of their differences in perception of the role itself.

■ *Intangibles*

The caseworker will often raise the point that in his analysis the research worker does not take into account the so-called intangibles and imponderables of the situation or the personality. But if the research worker does not take such factors into account, can we be certain that they are adequately accounted for in any intuitive approach? If factors are intangible, or even imponderable, how do we know that they exist? Can they be described in words or are they only felt? If they cannot be described in words, are they anything more than the observer's personal prejudices? What concordance is there between different observers equally concerned about imponderables or intangibles, and the ways in which they would communicate such concepts? Even if such factors do exist, is it not probable that they overlap with objective factors so that there is no point in dealing with them in their own right, assuming that they have such a right? The test which must be applied to these types of concepts is, of course, the test of effective communication. If a concept is so vague, so variable between persons, so imprecise that it cannot be communicated, then it is a private-language concept and has no claim to our attention. To be of any value at all, a concept must be communicable, and the message that the listener believes he received must bear some similarity to the message that the transmitter believes he has encoded and sent. The degree of convergence between the message transmitted and received can be subjected to various tests, based on methods that would normally be termed scientific. However, it is not known how the degrees of approximate similarity may be handled intuitively.

It seems in most cases that features which are said to be intangible are also incommunicable, especially when it is necessary for the decoded message to bear some similarity to the encoded message. Anything in this meaning of the term that is incommunicable can be no more than the private language or conceptual set of the observer. (The reduction to a unique language is an exactly similar procedure to that noted earlier in relation to the concept of the unique individual; see page 23.) Such private languages may have some function in terms of the individual's thought processes, but no one else has any way of knowing whether or not this is so. Therefore, we are not concerned with this form of encodification of concepts. Communication is an essential part of the method of scientific inquiry and of rational processes of decision-making. If a concept can be communicated, it can then be dealt with by means of the scientific method. Indeed, the nature of communication itself may be studied scientifically. In relation to some of the problems encountered in this field, it may be necessary to go through several processes of linguistic analysis before further progress can be made.

Much of the structure of belief regarding the outcome of penal treatment is derived from the "private language" of those concerned. No matter how experienced such persons may be, their knowledge is unsatisfactory, and their arguments will remain unconvincing until they can structure their concepts so that they conform to the generally accepted principles of communication of methods of inference.

BELIEF AND DISCOVERY

We are not stating that beliefs which cannot be directly supported nor feelings which cannot be communicated do not play a part in the development of scientific inquiry and in the discovery of new ways for the treatment of offenders. Beliefs can lead toward new discoveries, but they are not new discoveries in themselves. A belief may lead to the formulation of a hypothesis which can be subjected to test. If it survives the testing procedure, it may be held until a better one is found. If it does not survive, it should be interred by general agreement so that it does not further befog the issues, thus wasting research, social action, and administrative time. It follows that all informed persons should be able to agree to the rigor of the test procedures. Fortunately, there is more agreement as to what constitutes appropriate testing methods than there is to other aspects of social-science endeavor.

We shall not go into the complex questions of scientific method in any general philosophical way. However, it might be noted that it may be more reasonable to speak of progress in scientific knowledge by ways of disproofs rather than proofs. The layman often remarks: "You can prove anything by statistics," but the converse is true; it is possible to disprove statements but not to prove them. All truth is tentatively held. If research workers are unaware that certain hypotheses have been tested, research time will be wasted not only in redundant testing but also in the misdirection of thought processes and focus of the imagination. The results of evaluative research are thus as meaningful and necessary for the social-action worker and administrator as they are for the scientist, because it is from all those concerned with social problems that new developments may arise; the creative imagination is not restricted to only one sector of society.

RESEARCH PUBLICATION

A further deduction may be made from the preceding statement. Unless misdirected effort is part of a national-defense strategy (when it is presumed desirable to waste the enemy's resources), the communication of negative research results or policies is as important as the communication of positive results. Indeed, the definition of positive and negative results depends upon the particular observer's viewpoint. A scientist who is planning an experiment and who learns that what he proposes has previously been tried and has failed might regard such information as strongly positive. If research has been carried out with the necessary rigor, the results must be of value, no matter what the nature of the outcome. Only when research designs lack the necessary rigor have effort and money been wasted, and then it might reasonably be questioned whether the material should be published. Too often administrators take a different view of research publication, especially when they believe that so-called unsuccessful research (that is, research which did not demonstrate what the administration hoped) should not be published. Such might be the case, for example, if it were claimed that reduced caseloads for probation officers would be "certain" to facilitate the rehabilitation of the offender, and research failed to show this belief to be supported in the conditions specified.

Recently there has been a growing interest in research on the problem of caseload size. Some of these projects have utilized fairly sophisticated research designs (1). For our purposes here, it is sufficient to indicate that results have not supported the belief that the more attention given to a particular offender, the greater the chance that treatment will be successful. Caseload sizes have been modified very considerably without any significant changes in the rates of recidivism. There may be reasons for this which have not yet been discovered, but it is currently believed that the hypothesis is too simple which states that caseload size was a simple variable related to treatment efficiency and hence to effectiveness. Research results which show that caseload size is unrelated to recidivism might be used to support severe cuts in the probation program, and there could be arguments to suppress the results of such studies. Obviously, if all such results are suppressed because of the embarrassment they may cause to the probation or any other authorities, no progress could ever be made except within the organization to which the results were known. However, we are not concerned here with policy issues of this kind.

Problems derived from different viewpoints regarding criteria for the publication of research results are not without import in our present review of the state of knowledge in this field. (For an example involving unclear criteria, see page 40.) It would be expected that if twenty studies were carried out in a particular area and each were exactly similar, one would show significant results at the 5 percent level by chance alone. If enough studies were carried out to test a particular hypothesis and those that did not show a satisfactory or significant result were suppressed, anything could be proved. If pennies are tossed long enough, one will get five, six, ten, or even more heads in a row. If all other series are suppressed, one can supposedly prove that extrasensory perception influences the fall of the coin, or anything else, for that matter. With penny tossing this is obvious because we can assume the unknown frequency of nonreported tossings. If we wish, we may make our own reasonable assumptions when valid evidence is not provided. In other forms of research reporting, this is not as easy to do.

At present, it is not known what forms of editing or even suppressing of research results take place. In particular, evaluative research is too often sponsored by persons or authorities who have a particular interest in a specific outcome and an investment in the so-called proofs that might emerge. If public funds are made available to establish a new form of treatment for offenders or some variation in penal processes, those who apply for such funds believe that their ideas will work in practice. Support from those who provide the funds is usually related to the expected outcome rather than to the method of proposed investigation.

BIAS, CONSCIOUS OR UNCONSCIOUS

Bailey (4) has noted that the greater the degree of rigor in research studies, the less likelihood there is that such studies will show positive results, or indeed, results which indicate that treatment has any effect on outcome. Thus, repression of publication is only one way whereby the outcome of research may be concealed, and the administrator who withholds publication for political, personal, or practical reasons is not the only villain in this piece. Far from it. It is possible to make the criteria so unclear or to describe the procedures in such terms that the publication is, for all practical purposes, nonpublication. There are problems arising from mere incompetence, unbridled enthusiasms, economy, misunderstanding, and many other factors as well as political suppression of results which make interpretation of the state of knowledge hazardous.

There is too much emotional involvement in relation to the crime problem from those who clamor for protection from the offender and from those who believe that they are and indeed may be doing good; from those who advocate the "sick philosophy" of the criminal and from those who adhere to the simpler punitive approach. Whatever the viewpoint, the closeness of criminology and morals seems to result in dogmatic beliefs and a two-value logic obscuring all issues with thick coating of drama. It is necessary to separate moral considerations from the evaluation operation, and although these are separate issues, they have equal claims for attention. However, equal attention does not mean that they can be better attended to if they are totally confused and confounded into one heterogeneous mass (75).

4

Recidivists and recidivism

There has been much debate about the precise meaning of the terms "recidivist" and "recidivism." They derive from the idea of "backsliding"—a word often used in various religious literature. In criminology it is usual to refer to an offender as a recidivist when, after receiving treatment or punishment for an offense or group of offenses, he subsequently commits a new crime.

Some writers state that the term should not apply to offenders who commit only one subsequent offense after receiving treatment for their first offense—that is to say, offenders who commit only two offenses in total. Some have suggested that the total of two offenses is too strict a requirement and argue for three or even more offenses before classification as a recidivist. Preventive detention as used in England and Wales is reserved for those who have three or more offenses in certain categories beyond juvenile status. The conditions of qualification for preventive detention are somewhat complex, according to W. H. Hammond and E. Chayen (33). Preventive detention permits the court to take into account the prior record of the offender and his danger to society as well as the offense proved, and to sentence accordingly. Nonetheless, few offenders are so sentenced immediately upon qualification for this form of disposal. Similarly there has been discussion of the types of subsequent offenses which may be so trivial that they "should not count" toward the classification as recidivist.

For many purposes these kinds of arguments are themselves trivial, but in view of the fact that the classification of an offender as a "recidivist" may, in many jurisdictions throughout the world, make him liable for more serious punishment, there are legal aspects of considerable significance in the definition. The varying definitions of the information regarding the behavior of the offender influence the variety of the decisions which may be made by a court in respect of subsequent disposals for further crimes. Often the degree of seriousness of the criminal record is assessed in terms related to prior disposals by the courts. Thus a recidivist may be a person who has now committed a new crime (the crime itself often must be within a restricted set of categories) and who was previously committed to prison. Prior offenses which did not result in a court decision to commit to prison may not be counted as a qualification in the classification of recidivist.

THE COMMITMENT PROCESS—LABELS

In reviewing many of the studies on recidivism and recidivists it is often impossible to determine the restrictions on the definition. Few writers have included an investigation of the commitment process in connection with their studies of recidivists, but we shall note one exception to this. In addition to the impact of the classification as recidivist upon the disposal of the court, such classifications are often related to administrative procedures in handling the offender after he has been committed. In some countries special prisons or other institutions are specifically reserved for those whose record of offenses falls within the locally defined category of recidivist offender. Thus the consequences of the defining act are considerable, while the nature of the definition is itself a rather unsatisfactory one.

Clearly it is a matter of convenience for jurists to have some system of classifying offenders. From the decision-makers' view, the most obvious reference for classification may well seem to be related to those offenders who appear highly resistant to various attempts which have been made to reform them or to divert them from their criminal ways. The classification of an offender as a recidivist could be suggested to be related to the degree of criminal commitment his record may show, when, that is, the decision-makers are inclined to say that their patience is exhausted. The varying levels at which the cutting points are made in different countries may have something to do with national characteristics of tolerance and patience, but it has nothing to do with any discontinuity factor in the criminal career.

In some jurisdictions the term recidivist gives way to such value-laden terms as persistent offender or habitual offender. Whether the term "habit" can reasonably be applied to a particular form of behavior repeated only three or four times seems so doubtful that its use in this connection savors of a rhetorical overstatement ("You habitual criminal, you!") rather than a descriptive term. Similarly the term "persistent" suggests perseverance in the face of opposition, but in relation to common usage it may be more satisfactory. (For example, we refer to a "persistent stain" when we have tried two or three methods of removing it without success.) In either case, however, the reference is to the criminal and not to the treatment which he has received; *he* is habitual or persistent.

RESEARCH STUDIES

The term "recidivist" has many overtones relating to philosophies of treatment-punishment which we shall not treat here. As defined earlier, when the term is used here (unless related to a quotation from other works), it will simply mean that the offender, once treated-punished, has offended again and that the subsequent offense has been placed on his record.

Throughout the world there have been carried out hundreds, if not thousands, of studies of recidivists. Several schools of thought have grown up around those who have focused their attention merely on recidivists as persons rather than on any related processes or phenomena. In general, research workers have assumed that recidivists have by *their* conduct *defined themselves* as a specific type of offender worthy of special attention. In this they have followed, perhaps rather blindly, similar assumptions made by treatment and custodial authorities who have demonstrated their assumptions by provision of special institutions for these offenders.

The ease with which incarcerated offenders may be studied may not be a factor in the selection of projects which involve a captive audience, but it is a factor in the results. The captive audience may not be self-selected either directly or in the manner implied by the nature of the definitions, but there is a heavy selection factor present. It cannot be assumed that the recidivists who are found in the appropriate institutions are a sample of recidivists as such, and we shall note how this comes about in some detail. It will be immediately recognized, however, that studies of recidivists are not studies of the effects of treatment, although there may be some relationship between the two. It is most unfortunate that the distinction does not seem to have been recognized by even the majority of writers on this topic. What has been done to offenders, and particularly to those offenders variously labeled recidivists, has been assumed to be the direct outcome of *their* actions—in a simple cause-effect relationship. This has enabled the false logic to be accepted that the behavior of the recidivist provides sufficient definitions and that it has not been necessary to look any further into the defining processes.

■ *Familiar faces*

Studies of recidivists seem to have developed mainly out of the work of the philosophical, legal-orientated European schools of criminology rather than the more sociologically or psychologically orientated American schools. Naturally it is not surprising that those whose work entails the disposal of offenders through the courts or other legal processes should he impressed by the numbers of persons whom they see time and again. The familiar faces can make an impression out of proportion to their importance as a fraction of the total cases heard. Again, certain of the higher courts deal only with the more important (i.e., serious) cases. Thus the higher the level of the judicial officers concerned, the greater the bias of their personal sample of offenders toward the more heinous crimes. It seemed, perhaps, a rather natural question to ask in what ways those persons who appeared frequently before the courts differed from those who appeared with less frequency. Clearly those persons had not benefited as had others from the lessons which the courts had tried to teach them. It was obviously the process of learning which was to be questioned, not the processes of teaching.

Thus the direction of most inquiries has been toward the recidivist offender and what distinguishes him from other offenders, rather than the processes by which he has been identified as a recidivist or the impact of decision systems on the sample available in the establishments set aside for these persons. If the possible impact of identification and decision-making have not been considered particularly relevant, it is not surprising that the treatment afforded these offenders has not been closely examined. However, in the vast amount of work associated with many highly respected names in the criminological field, it is surprising that so little can be found which provides any assessment of the outcome of treatments.

The impressive array of researchers who have conducted studies of recidivism would seem to require additional attention here, but for reasons which may now appear almost self-evident, we shall gain no information of significance in terms of the evaluation of treatments as such from this investigation. Perhaps another reason for some attention to this area is the fact that where figures are available regarding rates of recidivism there appears to have been an increase. Whether this increase derives only from an increased efficiency with which records are maintained, or because there are more systems of information exchange, or for other reasons, it is not possible to state with any degree of confidence.

It has been suggested by specialists in this area that this line of study may be divided into two main categories: (1) the criminological-biological approach, and (2) the criminological-sociological approach. If these categories are reasonable, then it seems that midway between these two systems is the empirical study of what might be termed "criminal growth trends," as represented by the well-known work of R. Grassberger (32) and those who follow his school. The application of what have mistakenly been called prediction methods or the estimation of the probablity of recidivism is also related to this approach.

SOME IMPORTANT EARLY STUDIES
OF RECIDIVISTS

In the 1920's, the rival claims of environment and personality as explanations of human behavior were receiving considerable attention, while G. Aschaffenburg (3) was carrying out his study of recidivist offenders. Psychology was a new but already well-established discipline, and sociology was beginning to make itself vaguely felt. Concerns with philosophical issues of nature and nurture seem to have influenced many workers in the social and psychological areas at that time, and it is not surprising that criminals were selected as one group worthy of study because it was thought that light might be cast on the problems of causation in human behavior. Was heredity all-important or unimportant? Aschaffenburg explained the results of his study mainly in terms of an interaction between heredity and environment, and he directed attention to the factors of heredity, lack of education, poverty, and disease. He stressed the importance of the relationship between environment and disposition as the causal factor.

Philosophical arguments regarding the relative importance of personality and environment stimulated the thinking if not the methodology of most research workers in the field at the time. That the rival claims of nurture and nature were more noted in the criminological field than in other areas of human behavior was possibly due to the fact that the controversy was closely related to such concerns of jurisprudence as problems of free will and determinism and the related issues of culpability, responsibility, and *mens rea*. Dominant interests of this kind in the 1930's can be traced in the work of J. Schurich (59), E. Metzger (51), and K. Schnell (57). However while Metzger stated that it was meaningless to discuss whether predisposition or environment was the "cause of crime," he also said that the problem was to discover "to what extent the heredity predisposition or the influence of environment is to blame for the individual criminal act or the whole progress."

■ *Allocation of blame* (*responsibility*)

The need to find some factor or situation on which to blame the criminal act is noteworthy in Metzger and the work of the philosophical, legalistic European school of the period. The attempt to find something blameworthy is not the same as the attempt to find an explanation. The idea of explanation comes from the values of scientific inquiry, whereas the idea of responsibility and blame comes from the concepts of jurisprudence. The concepts of responsibility and blameworthiness do not appear to have had a salutary effect upon the development of hard, useful data in relation to the crime problem. Even if it were possible to allocate satisfactorily blame to some factor or person, knowledge of how the phenomena might be controlled or even predicted would probably not be further advanced.

As late as 1935, preoccupation with determinism and free will, and nature and nurture, were central to many criminological writers. K. Schnell (57) even went so far as to claim that he had solved this problem! Showing an excess of zeal and courage, he claimed that he had demonstrated that among recidivists, predisposition was more of a cause than environment. Further, he claimed to have shown that in the cases he studied, predisposition was causal in 80 percent and environment in 20 percent.

One year later a somewhat different twist was given to the personality argument by Wend, 1936 (70). Wend claimed that habitual criminals were either psychotic or degenerated characters. Whether the applications of these terms (or indeed any others like them) contribute anything additional to our knowledge of the environment, person, or problem than we knew before they were applied is very doubtful. If calling things names could solve problems, we would have few problems unsolved today. Wend set down the main characteristics of his sample of 394 recidivist offenders as follows:

1. There was early onset of the first criminal activity.
2. There was a short interval between crimes associated with severe penalties.
3. The methods and motives for the crimes appeared to be similar, and this was especially true in respect to larceny, fraud, and embezzlement.
4. There was close contact with so-called criminal society.
5. Crimes by serious professional criminals tended to have a greater geographical range in area of commission than for others.

■ *Samples—their selection*

Wend's work represented a notable approach to an empirical method in keeping with a new trend. His approach, and those of others like him at this time was, however, most unsatisfactory. Let us consider the results of Wend's study as noted above as a general example for many such studies. Wend obtained his recidivist offenders in an institution. Now consider the nature of a sample obtained in such an establishment: A prison may be regarded as some sort of container that holds offenders for differing lengths of time according to the term of sentence. Imagine a model of the prison as a physical container (such as a jug) with an input and output system. Objects are placed in the container and then discharged to the outside world. The time of retention within the container varies. Let us suppose that another mechanism is located outside the container that occasionally picks up the objects which have been discarded from the container and places them back into it again. A record is kept of the number of times and the period that each object is in and out of the container.

It follows that when we sample objects within the container at any point in time, the numbers in different categories of time spent in the container will be proportional to the length of time. Similarly, if we consider all objects that might be in or out of the container at the time of sampling, then the number sampled in each category of probability of being within the container will be proportional to the probability of their being inside at the time. For the greater total time that an object (recidivist) remains within the container (prison), there is a greater probability of being included at any time sampling should take place. Similarly, the greater the frequency with which objects are returned to the container, the greater is the probability that they will be included, should sampling be carried out. Thus, the total time that an offender-recidivist remains exposed to the risk of being drawn in any sample will, of course, also be dependent upon how frequently he is returned to the field of exposure. Thus, Wend's conclusion that recidivists demonstrate short intervals between crimes and tend to receive longer sentences might be nothing more than a characteristic of his method of sampling from the container (prison). The characteristics attributed to recidivists are not necessarily characteristics of recidivists at all, but characteristics of the sampling method in

relation to the system's input-output mechanism. Without appropriate adjustment or an entirely different sampling frame, no
statements can be made about recidivists by studies of a prison
population. Characteristics of a prison population may be studied
by sampling prison populations, but the characteristics of recidivists
must not be confounded with the characteristics of the sampling
method used for the purposes of research.

Should any reader wish to see for himself how this form of
sampling works, it is easy and interesting to simulate a prison population by use of some cards. Values are assigned to the cards
representing the previous criminal record; a sample is taken of
those outside the prison (initially this can be all the cards). A sentencing policy is simulated by arranging that those with the longer
criminal record (larger numbers) are placed in the pool representing the prison population for longer periods than others. New cards
are added simulating crimes proved and court disposals, each adding a number to the originally assigned value, and hence, qualify-
ing the card for longer periods of retention in the pool. Discharges
from the pool are at risk to selection for addition of a digit to the
existing number, together with those previously also outside the
pool. It is not long after the commencement of the series of input-
output operations that the pool begins to reveal very different characteristics from the total body of cards with which the operations began. Sampling from the pool can be seen to give very different results from sampling from the total population of cards,
and the characteristics of the majority of cards in the pool will
represent a reflection of the sentencing policy simulated.

■ *Evidence of what?*

From what is known of the sentencing policy of the courts, it would
appear that Wend's results showing that recidivists are characterized by "short intervals between crimes associated with severe
punishments" (2 above), does not appear to be a conclusion
which may be firmly made about recidivists as *persons,* but rather,
or at least, additionally, about the system of justice in which they
find themselves.

Consider the characteristics summarized under category 3
above—the "methods and motives for the crimes appeared to be
similar. . . ." Is it really suggested that the *modus operandi* index which is maintained by nearly all police forces does not have

any effect upon the mechanism which "picks up" the offenders who recidivate and places them in the "container"? If so, it is difficult to explain the use of this method of recording and the cost of the maintenance of the files. Clearly there must be a higher probability of detection and conviction with a consequent increase in the probability of a return to prison (and hence into Wend's sample) for offenders who lay themselves open to detection by further systems of detection—in this case, the *modus operandi* index. Thus, in respect to characteristic 3 we may have again a factor which does not relate to recidivists (persons) but to systems of detection —the input-output system of the institution which formed the sampling frame. Where the offender increases his probability of detection by the methods he uses in the commission of the crime or in subsequent behavior connected therewith (e.g., use of fences) whatever those methods of relation to the systems of detection, the probability of being drawn in a sample taken in an institution is similarly increased. Thus, these types of characteristics may apply to some types of recidivists, but there is no guarantee that the same characteristics apply to all recidivists. Police methods may vary from one area to another and such variations will show in the characteristics of the incarcerated populations, while it is clearly not valid to infer from the frequency of these characteristics that recidivists differ from one area to another.

In the particular study by Wend, it is possible that police methods of detecting offenders may have served to increase the probability of detection for those who were more frequently found in company with the so-called criminal society (category 4 above).

Of Wend's five categories, only two are possibly due to factors other than those generated by the method of sampling and its consequent reflection of the input-output system. There is no reason to suppose that the early onset of the first criminal activity should be related to detection methods, but it may be related to sentencing policy so that the length of time these offenders were consigned to an institution may have been greater, and hence the chance of their being drawn into the sampling system was also greater. It is not known whether such factors were taken into account by any of the judges who, by their decisions, created the population of recidivists studied. However, there is evidence from other studies which would indicate that those offenders who commence criminal activity when young and are also engaged in criminal activity later in life are among the worst risks for further recidivism.

■ *The life curves of offenders*

Before leaving the discussion of the earlier studies, reference should be made to an interesting departure from the prison-population sampling which was commonly used. In 1946, Grassberger (32), obtained a sample of 27,300 men who were *sentenced at least once* in the period from 1919 to 1937. It is not very clear from the report exactly how the sample was drawn, but the emphasis that the sample represented a high proportion of the 80,000 men sentenced in Austria during the period in question makes us suspicious of the rigor. Half of the crimes committed were apparently by first offenders who did not recidivate; property offenders showed a recidivism rate of about 60 percent and offenders guilty of violence against the person, 50 percent. A correlation between the probability of recidivism and the interval between offenses was noted—the shorter the interval between offenses, the greater the probability of recidivism at any time. These results are similar to significant results obtained from the more frequently used penal-institution populations.

Many of Grassberger's analyses are of interest in the light of later work. Although he himself examined his results to ascertain what he termed defects of disposition and used the same frame of reference that others of the European school had used, he also considered the possibility of a study of "life curves" of offenders. Without doubt, there is much of significance and utility in variations of this concept, but there are many pitfalls.

The concept of "life expectancy" is a valid and powerful actuarial method, but the extension of these methods to events that, at times, recur, is not as simple as many have assumed. Life and death processes have been subjected to considerable statistical research, and there are models among those available in the literature that are of use to the criminologist. It is also possible to use the statistical methods developed in connection with epidemiology and other stochastic process models. The choice of model depends upon the problem, and there is no single model which is "best" in a general way for various explanations in criminology. If we wish to obtain estimates of the probable size of the prison population at a given time, we should select methods that would most likely provide a reasonable answer. We might do better to utilize several different methods that relied upon different assumptions and then compare the results. If we wish to estimate what the likely effect will be in a given area on the number of crimes reported if more policemen are put on the beat, we would select a different model and utilize different basic data.

Perhaps the most interesting feature of Grassberger's work is that the significance of his different sampling method has not been noted by those who have commented on his results. The starting point of disposition by the court gives a much more interesting sampling frame than anything which may be found at later points in the system. After all, it is the decisions we wish to get right, and it is reasonable to begin with a sample of decisions. And, although Grassberger did not seem to notice it, this was what he sampled. It is true that these decisions were made about men, and he ignored decisions about women, but it would be a mistake to regard the sample as being one of persons, just as it is a mistake to regard a sample of prison inmates as a sample of persons; Grassberger's sample represents the initial decision in the chain of decisions, whereas the prison-population samples represent decisions and the nature of these decisions at many preceding points.

Certainly any information about the personalities of offenders or recidivists and inferences regarding their environmental situation cannot be determined on the basis of factors that merely change the probability of the offender finding himself within the catchment area of the net used by the research worker as a sampling frame, whatever that net might be. Studies of inmates in selected prisons or selected types of offenders (classified, for example, in terms of their current offense) are unsatisfactory. The very mechanism that caused them to be available for study in the particular prison or category includes at least correlates of the factors upon which estimates of the probabilities must be based. In different studies the methods of partitioning the information that the writers have chosen adjusted for one or more of the various biases introduced, but none have noted the general nature of the bias and made an over-all correction by weighting the initial probabilities of selection. In most countries data upon which many of the necessary weighting factors should be determined are not available.

Characteristics of offenders, indeed of all human populations, tend to be correlated with each other and to form patterns of factors. If, then, some of the characteristics that are assumed, in error, to be those of persons relate not to persons but only to the nature of the investigation's design, it is probable that all characteristics identified may relate in some way to the sampling system and perhaps only to that system. But this is not all; some of the characteristics *not* identified may be unidentified only because they are masked by the erroneous identification of those characteristics that derive directly from the method of sampling. Thus, it is not only what is claimed to be known that becomes suspect under conditions of poor sampling but also that which seems to remain unknown, and that which may appear to be demonstrated as untrue may in fact be true. In so many studies the sampling designs have been poorly worked out or poorly executed, and it is no wonder that so many studies in this field fail to support each other in their findings. The variety of the results may not only reflect the variety of the situations studied but may also reflect the various errors in sampling or methods of inference.

The foregoing argument does not mean that the use of institutional populations as sampling frames is in itself always an invalid procedure. There have been some excellent studies of prison populations from which many valuable inferences have been made regarding the nature of processes of institutionalization and inmate cultures. Such studies sample incarcerated persons and limit their inferences to incarcerated persons and the situations in which they are involved within the institutional environment. That is, they are concerned with the persons who are within the system, with the impact of the system upon them, and with like analyses. They do not presume to make statements about the nature of crime or criminals on the basis of samples of crimes or criminals where the probability of inclusion of any unit is proportional to some risk factor that remains unaccounted for. There is neither a generally valid nor invalid procedure; what is valid or invalid depends not upon the method but the method in relation to the logic of inference.

MORE RECENT STUDIES OF THE PROBABILITY OF RECIDIVISM

Despite sampling fallacies in most studies of recidivism, it is reasonably well established as a general factor that the probability of a person committing more offenses increases as the number of previous offenses increases, at least for persons whose criminal record is relatively short. But this is not a simple, direct relationship; it varies according to the offender's age as well as the prior record. One study that may serve as a model is *The Sentence of the Court* (61). Whether the results of this study can be expected to apply in any general way or not, the method is commendable.

This study related to obtainable information in respect to offenders in England and Wales, and the particular laws may have had some effect upon the results. The results are limited, and indeed the limitations were well selected and provide an important feature of the study's strength. There is a danger that simple, gross assessments may be misunderstood, but in order to make comparisons between the outcomes of different treatments, many factors had to be ignored, and clearly some of those excluded are important. Nonetheless, the study makes very clear the importance of the prior conviction record, and its joint effect with age, upon the probability of further offenses.

■ *Conditional probability*

Before presenting some of the more important results of this study, one or two further points must be noted in order that the contribution it made to the field may be appreciated. The simple fact that the likelihood of a further conviction tends to increase with prior convictions is true, but even this statement contains a slight modification of the form in which the results of recidivist studies are generally presented. The point of confusion is not complex in its logical form, but it involves complex mathematical operations if it is to be utilized, and, what is more important, the data must be arranged in a different manner from that normally employed in reconviction studies. It must be recognized that the probability of recidivism is not a meaningful probability, since it means the probability of the commission and detection of the $(n + 1)$ offense, where the value of n is unstated! Thus, any rational discussion of recidivism must take into account the fact that we are concerned with conditional probabilities, not simple probabilities. The probability of a second offense, *given* that the offender has committed only one, is different from the probability of a fourth offense *given* that the offender has committed three, and so on. The necessity of the "given" may seem self-evident, but in talking about "recidivists" as though they were a class of persons, the necessary *given*

is not given, and frequently not even disclosed. It is also desirable
to consider the probability of a fourth offense, *given* that the offender has committed, say, one, two or three prior offenses, and so
on for any number of offenses in the series either real or imaginary.

   In Figure 1 (reproduced from *The Sentence of the Court*) is
shown a family of similar curves of recidivism rates for different
age groups. The very considerable effect of age will be immediately obvious. A first offender in the age group 8–16 years, for ex-

FIGURE 1. *Reconviction according to offender's age
and previous convictions*
(Percentage reconvicted within five years)

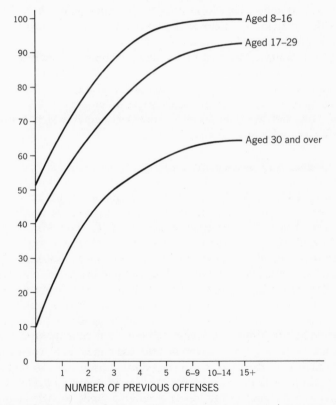

SOURCE: *The Sentence of the Court,* Home Office Report. London: H.M.S.O., Code
34–433–O–66, 1964. Reprinted by permission of the Controller of Her Britannic
Majesty's Stationery Office.

ample, has a probability of being convicted of another offense of about 65 percent, while the similar probability for a person in the age group 17–29 is 55 percent, and for the age group of 30 years and older, the same probability drops to about half, namely 28 percent. This result may seem surprising. It is generally believed that older persons are less capable of changing their ways or of benefiting from treatment. Empirical data, however, suggest that it is the older offenders who are, criminal record for criminal record, far *better* risks than the younger offenders. It may be that the older person experiences more social consequences from his act than the younger person, whatever the disposal of the court, or perhaps there are a large number of reasons at present unknown. Nor is it known to what extent similar results would be found in other cultures and under other legal systems. It seems highly likely, however, that something similar would be found to apply in most technologically developed countries.

The generalized curve of probabilities in Figure 1 applies to all types of court action in the disposition of cases. This provides a simple form of expectation or a generalized average of recidivism. Varieties of treatment might make some differences in the recidivism rate, and we shall have to consider studies which address themselves to this more complex task later.

■ *Limited concordance in results*

In 1964, S. Kogi, Y. Ishikawa and J. Sugamata (39) conducted an intensive search of the literature regarding studies of recidivism. Covering nearly one hundred studies from C. Lombroso (42), G. Aschaffenburg (3), and A. Lenz (40), to current work, they noted that generally recidivism was said to be more probable when the criminal career began early in life, and that the more committed the offender was to crime, the more likely it was that he would continue. The degree of concurrence between so large a number of studies on these two factors is interesting, as is the fact that there seems to be a lack of concurrence with respect to other factors.

Kogi, Ishikawa, and Sugamata also used their analyses to develop their own theory of the infraction of prison rules in relation to the prior conviction record, but there is no reason to believe that behavior within the institution is a reliable guide to behavior on discharge. It is certainly unreasonable to substitute for the criterion of recidivism some criterion relating to behavior in the prison as a point of reference for the research analysis. Prison discipline is one matter which may be studied in its own right and for its own purposes, but the general public is more concerned with behavior after discharge.

■ *Treatment variants*

As an example of a study of recidivist offenders (as defined in the English law) we may refer to W. H. Hammond, and E. Chayen (33). The authors appreciated that the outcome of treatment could not be assessed without reference to the selection for treatment. It appears that they were asked to study a form of penal treatment (or nontreatment) known as "Preventive Detention." This is a long-term incarceration which may be awarded to qualified offenders. The qualification is somewhat complex, but amounts to three prior offenses of a certain type, committed after a certain age, and dealt with in certain specific ways in the past by the courts. Three prior minor offenses would not normally qualify a fourth-time offender for preventive-detention sentence, and it is interesting to note that an offender on the occasion of his disposal by a court for that offense which would, on the next occasion qualify for "P.D." must be notified of this fact. The idea of this procedure presumably being that it will add to the deterrent effect of the lengthy P.D. term.

Hammond and Chayen studied those offenders who had in fact been committed to preventive detention as well as a group of similarly qualified offenders who were otherwise disposed of. They showed that the courts did in fact tend to select offenders for preventive detention based on certain characteristics in terms of the offenders as persons and in terms of their prior records of offenses. Only a small proportion of those who qualified for preventive detention were in fact awarded it at any time and hardly any at the first occasion of their appearance in court after qualification.

In these circumstances it is perhaps not surprising that Hammond and Chayen reported they could trace no effect of the deterrent official warning regarding qualification, nor indeed did their results in this special sector of the offender population show findings any different from other equally rigorous studies of other offender groups. Little or no differences could be found to be related to the very different forms of treatment awarded to the qualified recidivist offender, whether given preventive detention or otherwise disposed of by the courts.

The particular interest of this study is its attempt to evaluate different forms of preventive detention, one of which was a type of halfway-house treatment. The system may be described briefly as follows: A sentence of preventive detention may consist of two or three stages. The selection for the third stage has many similarities with a parole system, although strictly speaking, the prison system in England and Wales did not have a parole provision when the study was conducted.

Stage 1 consists of a comparatively short period served under ordinary conditions in a local prison. This is followed by a less rigorous form of imprisonment with a higher standard of living, served in a central prison to which the offender is allocated [after 1956 by special allocation centers].

Stage 2 lasts until the offender appears before a Special Advisory Board for selection to Stage 3, and during this time there is the disciplinary sanction of return to Stage 1.

Stage 3 has many more amenities and serves as a prerelease training, during which the prisoner receives vocational training and other training for his future after discharge. This involves working outside the prison, and where practicable, it should include a period spent in a hostel, living a life as near normal as possible. Offenders in Stage 3 normally get one-third remission and the training begins about twelve months before this time. Offenders not selected for Third Stage serve five-sixths of their sentence; initially these men did not have any prerelease training, although more recently many have been able to spend their last six months in huts within the prison walls while undertaking work outside the prison under supervision [33, page 10].

It will be noted that the main difference (at least from the prisoner's viewpoint) is that if he can obtain Stage 3, his period in detention is considerably shortened. From the taxpayer's point of view, the cost of retaining in detention is considerably less for those who are placed in Stage 3. There may be said to be some "real" differences between the two forms of treatment.

The authors of the study were able to distinguish characteristics of preventive detainees who were more or less likely to be awarded Stage 3 by the advisory board, but (on page 142) they report: "There is a very close correlation between the board's allocation and most of the information given them by the prison, yet despite this and the board's agreement with the staff prognosis, the selection was not successful in distinguishing those who were later reconvicted." In other words, there was no difference between the selected cases given selective treatment and those not selected.

According to the study, the board tended "to take note of the offender's previous record; fraud offenders, offenders aged 30–39, or those who had been on probation and those with fewest previous convictions were most often put on third stage." There were also some other considerations which the board considered to be of significance.

Is the lack of any correlation between the treatment and the outcome, a deficiency of the selection machinery, as the authors seem to suggest? Or is third-stage treatment in fact so much better that the same results are obtained for selected persons with a reduction in time and cost of detention? Or is the treatment worse in the third stage, and does the board's selection mask this effect because it is selecting better risks? From the study's design it is impossible to know which of these explanations is the more probable.

Despite the fact that the treatments did not have any apparent relation to outcome—or the interactions were so complex that they could not be separated by a study of this kind—Hammond and Chayen were able to obtain some powerful prediction equations which discriminated between the better and worse risks within this highly selected group of adult recidivists.

5

Prediction methods

In few fields of inquiry, even in the behavioral sciences, are separate areas claimed for the application of a particular method of analysis. No claims are made for any special treatment of multiple regression in psychology or sociology. It is doubtful that in any other area of study would anybody think it worthwhile to try establishing a school of thought identified only by the fact that a particular group of statistical or quasi-statistical techniques had been applied to a problem within the field concerned. Yet in criminology so-called prediction methods have been given a special place. Is this due to the particular nature of the subject matter? Is such a special place justified? In what ways do prediction methods differ from other methods in relation to the problems to which they may be applied? Perhaps prediction methods attained their importance in criminology not because of their value or power or because of any special characteristics of the subject matter or the method, but rather because of the special characteristics of those who advocated their use.

Emphasis upon the prediction method as a particular aspect of criminology has been disadvantageous for development of the subject. To some extent all scientific methods are concerned with prediction, but not in the same way as most criminologists have suggested with respect to their prediction tables. In other fields (not always so in criminology) the predictability is sought not for its own sake, but as a means toward the solution of certain specific problems, as an aid to the understanding of issues, and as a tool to facilitate control of phenomena. Many criminologists have missed the whole point of the statistical method as a general approach to a wide range of problems by emphasizing prediction methods without precisely stating what the prediction was for.

PREDICTION AND INFERENCE

It is now coming to be realized that, even if prediction methods are worthy of a separate place in the literature of the subject, they are not appropriately titled. If the term "prediction" means anything, it cannot refer to a method of analysis. The predictions that may be made are made by inference by persons on a basis of evidence of varying quality and type, and the methods for dealing with these types of data may vary widely. In practice rather motley collections of statistical methods have been used in so-called prediction studies. Both methods and the predicted situations vary, and there is no single method that qualifies as *a* prediction method. Moreover, the problem that one might assume underlies the desire and attempt to predict has often been lost sight of in the process.

DELINQUENCY AND RECIDIVISM PREDICTION

The main class of studies listed under the heading "prediction methods" falls into two distinct groups. The first attempts to predict recidivism, and the tables produced were assumed to be of value in providing guidance for the parole boards' decisions in cases of indeterminate sentences. The second class of prediction methods is those that attempt to predict the likelihood that a young person (such as a child who has not been found guilty of an offense) may at some future time become an adjudicated delinquent or criminal. The similarity between these two classes of prediction is superficial, for there are considerable differences in the required methodology and seriously different problems in relation to the moral questions involved. For the present, let us limit our attention to the first class. These studies would better be designated as providing experience tables, or tables of base expectancy, or perhaps even more appropriately, estimates of the probability of recidivism, rather than prediction. Thus, for example, we might have estimates of the presentence probability of recidivism, or postrelease estimates of the probability of recidivism, and the like. In the first example the tables would refer to estimates of likely recidivism after treatment as made on the basis of evidence before the court had disposed of the initial case.

■ Prediction not personality assessment

The types of problems that may be enlightened by the different forms of tables are naturally widely different. The quantity of information available upon which to base the estimates of probability also differs according to the period at which the estimation is to be made. At the time of discharge from prison it is possible to take into account the behavior of the offender during his period of training, whereas in the presentence estimates this information is not available. In no way can the estimates of probability of recidivism be assumed to apply directly to the person as a kind of personality measurement. Certain tests that purport to measure aspects of personality may be associated with recidivism, but that is a different matter. It is to be expected, pending evidence to the contrary, that the estimates of recidivism (or anything else) will vary as some function of the available and utilized information in deriving the estimates. Thus, an estimate of recidivism made at the point of discharge will be more powerful than one made before entry into the treatment process but less accurate than one made after the offender had completed one year crime-free after release.

One further although perhaps very elementary point, must be stated before we consider the work that has been done in this area. While they are not *predictions,* estimates of probabilities may be used *as* predictions if this is desired, but they can also be put to other and perhaps more valid use.

The prediction school represents a tragedy rather than a disaster for criminology. The approach had great promise and potential; indeed, modifications of the basic methods still represent one of the best and most feasible approaches to the evaluation of treatment. The tragedy lies in the fact that the methods were not quickly developed from their early naïve stages but remained almost static for some thirty years. Disaster lies in the confusion between the prediction of recidivism and the prediction of probable juvenile delinquency. Yet even the crudest prediction methods require the following-up of cases for a considerable period of time. In this they revealed the necessity for information regarding outcome of treatments, and thus, their contribution to operational thinking and research has been a positive one, even where the methods were weak and the techniques heavily oversold.

HISTORICAL NOTES ON PREDICTION METHODS

Some so-called prediction methods are nothing more than crude weighting devices for items of information found to be related to recidivism. Many of the proposed systems do not meet the requirements for the valid construction of scales or scoring. In this section we shall consider samples of those studies that claimed prediction as the aim, irrespective of the method employed to provide the estimate of the probability of recidivism or the method of stating such estimates.

■ *First prediction study*

The first prediction study in criminology is usually attributed to one made by S. B. Warner (68), who published his paper in 1923. Warner carried out his study at the suggestion of Sanford Bates, who at that time was the Massachusetts Commissioner of Corrections. Warner based his study on 680 prisoners in the Massachusetts State Penitentiary. The sample was formed from 300 inmates who were subsequently successful on parole, 300 subsequent violators, and 80 who were not paroled. The whole sample had appeared before the parole board between 1912 and 1920. Warner classified 64 items of information available in their records and used these data to compare the three groups. Warner did not go on to construct any prediction tables but used his data to consider the criteria employed by the parole board as a basis for its decision to grant or deny parole. In this way Warner avoided many of the errors of subsequent workers.

(It is interesting to note that much early work in criminology was more soundly based than much subsequent work, because earlier research workers were more aware of the limitations of their approach.)

The criteria used by the board at the time of Warner's study (68) were:

1. Whether the man had supposedly profited from his stay in the institution and had so far reformed that it was unlikely he would commit another offense
2. His conduct in the institution
3. Whether suitable employment was awaiting him on release
4. Whether he had a home or other proper surroundings to go to
5. His ability to tell the exact truth when interviewed by the board
6. The seriousness of his offense and the circumstances surrounding it
7. His previous criminal record
8. The appearance he made before the board in applying for his parole
9. Behavior on former parole

Based on his comparative figures for violators and nonviolators, Warner demonstrated that most of the criteria used by the board in making judgments were without foundation. For example, the board regarded the commission of a sexual offense as unlikely to be a good prognosis (criterion 6), but in actual fact two-thirds of the paroled sex offenders proved successful against a total success rate of about one-half. Prisoners committed for larceny and breaking, who were most usually regarded as good parole risks, had a violation rate of 57 percent. Warner's early findings on this have subsequently been demonstrated as generally true and applicable in a number of countries, some of which have quite different cultural patterns.

In the light of developments in criminology, it is notable that Warner was concerned with the decision processes of the Parole Board and not with prediction in its own right, nor indeed did he emphasize this idea. If others had kept his early focus of relating information to decisions, this area might have had a more healthy development. However, soon after Warner's work had been published it began to attract criticism, possibly on the least significant grounds. One of his critics, Hornell Hart (34), suggested that Warner might have constructed a prediction table by using a system of weights for different items. Although Hart made this suggestion, he himself did not construct one. Furthermore, his suggestion may have begun an interest in prediction that later diverted development from concern with the nature of the decision process toward more abstract ideas of prediction instruments.

Another major criticism that Hart made on Warner's work was that among the 64 items Warner used, 15 discriminated between violators and nonviolators to the 1 percent level of statistical significance. Hart in turn was criticized and was accused of accepting evidence obtained directly from prisoners when it suited his purpose and rejecting it when it conflicted with his views of previous criminological findings. On this point, Warner had criticized the board for relying on evidence derived from the prisoners. He noted that in about half of the factors used in decision-making on such information as family backgrounds, education, habits, and circumstances at the time of the crime—were obtained by questioning the offender. Warner concluded that apart from the psychiatric report there was little information of value in case papers.

Thus, the beginnings of prediction were characterized by controversy, and even today there is a notable lack of agreement in criminology regarding this area of work, both by those who construct such tables and seek to defend them and by those who might be expected to use the information. In some cases the criticism is helpful in developing the methods, but much of it is ill-informed and based on ignorance of statistical methods and systems of inference. Naturally there is scope for disagreement, but there is also much that cannot be debated without rejecting the whole philosophy of the scientific approach. There is room for debate on the uses of prediction but less room for debate in respect to many of the methodological issues.

In 1928, E. W. Burgess (11), then with the University of Chicago, produced the first prediction table in the form in which it is now recognized, while investigating the working of the indeterminate-sentence law and the Illinois parole system.

Burgess noted at the state penitentiary in Joliet that the general rate of parole violation, which was 28.4 percent, was considerably higher for offenders convicted of fraud or forgery, who showed a violation rate of 42.4 percent. Murderers and those convicted of manslaughter, on the other hand, showed a reconviction rate of only 9 percent. Burgess produced a prediction table by allocating a weight of one point to each factor associated with failure, and favorable (or negative) points for factors associated with success. The individual cases were then scored, and a table of expectancy rates of parole violation and nonviolation was constructed. The table seemed remarkably successful and showed, for example, that among men with between 16 and 21 favorable points, only 1.5 percent violated, whereas for men with only 2 to 4 favorable points the rate of violation was 76 percent. Perhaps Burgess' method of weighting may be regarded as the one that has been most widely used to date in techniques of criminological prediction table construction.

■   *Sheldon and Eleanor Glueck*

The Gluecks (26, 27), whose internationally famous researches began almost simultaneously with Burgess, utilized the magnitude of the correlation with success or failure as the weight in their prediction tables. Superficially, this appears to be a more sophisticated approach, but as we shall show, it is doubtful that it represents any improvement upon Burgess' simpler system, and both are unsatisfactory.

The first study by the Gluecks was *Five Hundred Criminal Careers* (26). This is based on a careful investigation into the life histories of all prisoners released from the Massachusetts reformatory whose sentences expired in 1921–1922; there were 510 such cases. A follow-up period (of at least five years) occurred between the expiration of their sentences and the beginning of the investigation in 1927. In many cases the period of follow-up was much longer, because a large number of men had left the institution before the expiration of their sentence. This additional follow-up period is often cited as a positive feature of the research. However, it should be noted that a follow-up period is also a period of exposure to risk for the offender. It is to be expected that the longer the period of exposure to risk, the greater the likelihood of reconviction, if all other things are equal, and they certainly are not. Therefore, a confused period of follow-up or exposure to risk is clearly no advantage, nor indeed is there any advantage in a period that varies extensively with regard to dates and hence in the conditions of the world in which the offender is released. Of the 510 cases, 51 percent left the institution in 1917–18 and another 17 percent in 1919–20.

The Gluecks were well aware of the unreliability and incompleteness of much of the information in official files, and they carefully checked and supplemented their material from other sources. In 73 percent of their cases the former prisoners or close relatives were interviewed by an experienced fieldworker to check and supplement material and to obtain a picture of subsequent adjustment.

As we have noted, the Gluecks constructed their prediction tables by reference to the items that had the highest coefficients of contingency. The six most highly related prereformatory factors were: work habits ($C = 0.42$), seriousness and frequency of prereformatory crimes ($C = 0.36$), arrest for crime preceding the offense for which sentenced to the reformatory ($C = 0.29$), penal experience prior to reformatory sentence ($C = 0.29$), economic responsibility preceding sentence to reformatory ($C = 0.26$). However, the total score showed a correlation of only 0.45, which is only 0.03 above that of the prognosis obtained from only a single factor, prereformatory work habits, reported as 0.42. The gain of 0.03 using six items of information instead of one is certainly not significant, and there is also considerable cost in obtaining information that has no additional power.

Perhaps the reason for the inefficiency of the total score lies in the system of weighting the factors. The score was obtained by adding up the lowest percentage of total failures that were characteristic of a particular tabulation and then adding two more score classes between the two extremes. Thus, the Gluecks attempted to give effect to A. B. Vold's (65) criticism by giving greater weight to factors more strongly correlated with success or failure. It seems that they did not recognize that weighting by each factor in accord with its zero-order correlation and then in percentage terms was most unlikely to provide an efficient combined score. For example, consider the item with the major single power, referred to as work habits ($C = 0.42$), and compare it with the factor of economic responsibility preceding sentence to reformatory. How are these two factors distinguished? Will the first be expected to contribute any further information in the presence of the latter? As the total score correlation shows, not only did this second counting of something related to work add nothing, but neither did the other four items. Methods for adding information together to get more power in total are complex, and we shall return to this question in Chapter 14.

The same group of offenders as constituted the basic data for *Five Hundred Criminal Careers* (26) was followed up for another five years, and the results were published under the title *Later Criminal Careers* (27). After another five years they were again reported upon, in *Criminal Careers in Retrospect* (28). Thus, in all, this particular group of offenders had a total of over fifteen years of follow-up.

Reference cannot be made here to all the developments between these early beginnings and the present. It may, however, be noted that although prediction was developed so that it could be applied in connection with release on parole, there are in fact very few cases where such methods have had practical use. This omission may suggest that the practical men in the field of sentencing and treating of offenders were uncertain as to the rigor of the research workers' methodology. It also seems that what may have been the right decision not to use prediction tables was made on irrelevant issues.

The parole decision does not itself indicate the nature of the background information required to facilitate rational action. But prediction workers seem to have taken too simple a view of the process and to have sought answers to inappropriate questions, albeit with more rigor. The decision process itself has only recently come under study.

DEFICIENCIES OF EARLY PREDICTION WORK

It seems safe now to conclude that the early prediction tables represent an attempt to answer the wrong questions, and to do so by a means that could not be described as efficient.

The research workers' acceptance of inappropriate questions for study is unfortunate but not entirely their fault. The questions that were being asked seemed important at the time, and they might have provided a good starting point. Sheldon and Eleanor Glueck and others with them, however, not only accepted the questions as useful and correct but staked much on extension of the questions as background for their philosophy. Only recently have research workers begun to challenge the basic assumptions of perceptions of "need." Earlier it seems to have been believed that if the future could only be predicted, there would be no difficulty in deciding upon the best action to take (72, Chapter 2). But of course it does not follow that a knowledge of the future will automatically indicate the best current policy, nor is there a possibility of complete prediction. The questions that it might have been more scientific to investigate relate to what it might have been more profitable, humane, or economical to do, and to the critical points at which action could best be taken. Instead, attention was devoted to attempting to answer questions as to what the outcome might be, irrespective of any decisions then being made. The emphasis was placed upon the determination of cause-effect relationships linked with a failure to recognize the importance of situation and process.

■ *Validation*

It is remarkable that despite a tradition in behavioral research for all test materials to be validated upon samples different from those used in the construction of any test, prediction tables have almost without exception lacked this safeguard. Where validation has been claimed, it has been only partial. Such partial validation may be more unsatisfactory than none. It must be noted that in any prediction there will be two classes of error (for a more detailed discussion of error see Chapter 12):

1. Some offenders will be "predicted" as recidivists (or delinquents) who will, in fact, subsequently *not* become delinquent or recidivist.
2. Some offenders will be "predicted" as nonrecidivists (or nondelinquents) who will, in fact, subsequently become delinquent or recidivist.

In any assessment of the validity of the prediction both kinds of error must be considered. It is not sufficient to show that among recidivists, a high percentage could have been predicted without also showing for nonrecidivists the percentage who would also have been correctly classified.

Taking a sample of offenders and showing that a large proportion would have scored in the delinquent category does not validate the prediction. Yet claims of this kind are frequently found. If decisions are made upon the basis of prediction statements, it is to be expected that the consequences of errors in each class will be different. It may be more damaging to regard (predict) a person as delinquent or recidivist when this is incorrect, than to incorrectly regard a person as nondelinquent or nonrecidivist. Some recent writers have claimed that the first kind of error can lead to a self-fulfilling prophecy—the labeling process of classification as "likely delinquent" may change the perception of the person by others, and through this, his own self-image.

■ *Limits of utility*

A further error in the prediction method found to apply generally (until very recent years) to studies reported was the failure to recognize that the sample of offenders which provided the basic information determined at the same time the limitations of valid interpretation. A general truth cannot be established on the basis of information obtained from a sample that is not representative of the population about whom it is desired to make inferences (e.g., predictions). This means that where the prediction tables were based on information obtained from the output of one prison or penal system, there is no reason to suppose that the findings should hold for any other prison or penal system, or even to the input of the same prison. Only under certain conditions can it be assumed that the characteristics of a sample of output are sufficiently equal to a sample of input. Because the penal system is not a static system, it is very unlikely that information regarding a sample of output would be equal or sufficiently similar to the same information obtained in respect to a sample at the time of input. A decision made at the time of output in relation to members of the output population might be assisted by careful analysis of data obtained from a sample of the output. Decisions made, or inferences regarding factors relating to input are not so certainly facilitated by information obtained at output, but would require input-based information.

Thus, the emphasis of early prediction values on the relationship between the decision process and information that could be available was more appropriate than that which developed soon after. Many students seemed to assume that the prediction method would arrive at some immutable "causes" that by some means would be independent of the sample design and uninfluenced by either the time or place of the research. Some results have, it has turned out, proved somewhat invariate. For certain purposes this lack of variance is an interesting and useful characteristic of some types of measurement. Whether those factors that are characterized by greater stability are nearer so-called truth than others that show greater variability is not a sophisticated question.

■ *Decisions and predictions*

When Burgess and Warner studied data directly related to a decision system, they were on safer ground than the later prediction workers. The decision and sample were the same reference group for Burgess and Warner. Errors of the first and second kind would occur regardless of the means by which predictions were made—statistically or subjectively. Others who followed them quickly stepped from firm ground into a mire of complex pitfalls. In addition to the major errors, namely, those of faulty sampling designs (or errors in relation to the nature of the inferences made) failure to recognize two types of error as possibly having different consequences, and poor weighting of the scores, one or two other faults should perhaps be indicated.

Most critics of prediction workers, notably of the Gluecks, base their attack upon the inefficiency of the methods of weighting. These criticisms are not matters of opinion but can be demonstrated to hold. Nonetheless, the tables prepared by the Gluecks continue to appear to work. How can a method which can be attacked on so many grounds seem to work in practical situations and to hold in different parts of the world? In some cases the explanation is rather simple—the errors committed in earlier work have also been replicated in subsequent work.

A. A. Walters (67), pointed out one basic error involved in matching samples as used for prediction-table construction in 1955–1966. This criticism is another form of the criticism that the samples used do not mirror the population for which the predictions are supposed to be required. C. Banks, in 1964 (7), provided a thorough analysis on the basis of certain assumptions regarding the population percentage of expected delinquents, using tables provided by both the Gluecks (29) and by D. H. Stott, 1960 (60). These criticisms apply more directly and simply to predictions of delinquency rather than to recidivism, but the general questions remain similar. On the safe assumption that about 17 percent of the population could be delinquent (perhaps a 50 percent increase on the best estimates for England and Wales), she observes, "If we had classified *all* of the 890 children as *not* delinquent we should have been wrong in 151 cases (i.e., 17 percent), but using the figures from the Glueck Social Prediction Scale, we should have been wrong in 191 cases (21 percent of the total)." This is because in the tables in *Unravelling Juvenile Delinquency* 451 children were delinquent and 439 were not delinquent. In other words, the sample as designed had about 50 percent delinquent, but in few real populations will there be such a high percentage of delinquent children.

In reconviction studies, perhaps fortuitously, because a recidivism rate of about 50 percent is frequently observed, the balancing of the sample may not represent such a serious problem. But other errors have been substituted. In tables on both recidivism and the prediction of delinquency, the Gluecks and others like them have used items that were mainly subjective assessments of habits or characteristics of the persons sampled. But not only are subjective assessments made at the prediction stage, they are also the basis for the decisions that relate to the criterion. Some element of prophecy may not be prophecy at all but a carry-forward of the initial type of basic element underlying the two separate independent subjective assessments. In other words, the decision of the schoolteacher who may be making the "prediction" rating of "stability of home background" may be influenced by features similar to those observed by persons who may be looking for suspects in a crime. Clearly when an attempt is made to clear up a crime, not all members of the population are equally suspect—and, indeed, this is altogether sensible. However, the proportion of crime cleared up is small in comparison with the total number of crimes known to the police, varying from about 25 percent to seldom more than 50 percent, and this variation is related to the types of offenses known to be committed. Is there not at least a possibility, if not a reasonably high probability, that those who are indirectly rated as "suspect" at the time of prediction appear to have similar characteristics to those who are later more directly suspected?

In the Glueck studies this possibility of a self-fulfilling prophecy is enhanced by the fact that they do not accept external evidence of subsequent criminality without editing. Some who are in fact convicted or reconvicted are, for other reasons, at times classified as "successes," while others who have escaped conviction or reconviction are rated as "failures."

The use of "soft" data—ratings and other forms of subjective judgments for which replication by other workers is always difficult and doubtful—makes it impossible to test the reliability of much prediction work, even if it were otherwise sound.

No prediction is proved by the same data that were used to establish it in the first place. Yet, as we have noted, in very few cases have validation studies been made or even attempted. Where sound validation studies have been attempted, the power of the prediction has dropped markedly, especially in cases where the prediction was based on subjective assessments.

6

Summary reviews of treatment and its effects

Although it has been possible for some time to see how evaluation could be developed in the penal-treatment field, little serious work has yet been attempted. Few administrations are prepared to put money into research concerning the treatment of offenders, and although there are a few notable exceptions, even these are of recent origin. The pattern for research and evaluation as it is now seen is closely related to the work of the 1950s. More recently there have been a few developments in methods for the analysis of problems in criminology and a number of surveys on the state of knowledge. Some excellent information retrieval systems have also recently been established. Criminological research is becoming an aspect of national significance in the United States. What has been the nature of this growth, and how do those who have viewed the general scene assess the position?

INSTITUTION STUDIES

One interesting fact to be noted from the searches of the literature is that while studies of criminals, recidivists, juvenile delinquents, and deviants abound, there is a poverty of material discussing and describing different types of treatments. Exactly what goes on in prison, what takes place in group counseling, what a probation officer does and similar questions have not been given much attention. In this sector we have had to rely mainly upon the work of former inmates whose views may not be representative, because the proportion of inmates who have written books and found publishers is extremely small and atypical of the majority. Few if any of the works describing treatment processes seem to consider that there is any remedial effect in the components of the prison or other systems. Of course the public demands other features in the penal system than the therapy of treatment, and these demands must be considered in the type of system provided. But exactly how much security does the public obtain at how much unit cost? What is a "unit"? What is meant by "cost"? These would seem to be important questions, but apparently they have seldom been asked, and few attempts to answer them can be traced.

■ *One hundred studies examined*

There has been much more concern with the outcome of prison treatment than with what goes on inside the institution. This stage may be passing as certain forms of experimental work begin to be developed. Several hundred studies of outcome were published in English in the twenty years from 1940 to 1960. The U.S. Health Service recently sponsored a large-scale investigation of the literature of correctional outcome studies. Walter C. Bailey (4) and his associates examined 100 such reports, which they classified according to methods utilized and outcomes reported. Bailey recorded: 22 experimental studies; 26 systematic empirical; 52 nonsystematic empirical. It is not without some regret that it is to be noted that the treatment outcome that he classified as "harmful or no effect" increased from 4 percent for the nonsystematic group to 23 percent for the group classified as experimental. Only 9 of the studies reported results that were claimed to be statistically significant; but, as is noted later, some of these were significant only in the statistical sense, because of the method of defining outcome. Bailey concluded that "the effects of wishful thinking become progressively less controlled as the rigor of research design decreases."

It is not known whether the 100 studies that formed Bailey's sample were in any way representative of all recent correctional outcome studies, and, what may be more important, how representative his sample was of correctional procedures. An element of conscious selection must be expected in the selection for assessment by means of a research project of a certain form of treatment. Are such selected procedures representative or are they more likely to represent treatments that are believed to be "good" treatments? Is it likely that research workers would be asked to evaluate a treatment program that was believed to be no more than average? Bailey further noted that "evidence of the effectiveness of correctional treatment is inconsistent, contradictory and of questionable reliability." Unless we are to believe that uninvestigated correctional procedures are generally superior to those investigated among the 100 projects, his conclusion is most disturbing. Perhaps on the evidence supplied by Bailey we might conclude that most or all correctional treatments are increasing rather than decreasing the probability of recidivism.

On the evidence set forth by Bailey, the hypothesis that all or most correctional treatment programs are harmful cannot be rejected. This hypothesis is not to be lightly dismissed as nonsense, nor is it a simple matter to test. By reason of the philosophy of jurisprudence and the practice of law, *something* must be done about the offender, and it is not possible to permit spontaneous recovery as an alternative to action. The problem of selection of treatment may reduce to the selection of the form of disposal that has the least amount of content, since all content is likely to have undesirable effects. By doing as little as possible we may be doing as little harm as possible. The best (but illegal) treatment for offenders may be a placebo!

■ *British survey*

It may be claimed that this analysis is a little too hard on the studies examined and that this may be the result of a particular enthusiasm for rigorous research that this writer apparently shares with Bailey. But Bailey is not alone in coming to conclusions of the kind reported above, nor does all the evidence of this type come from the United States. The Baroness Wootton of Abinger (Professor Barbara Wootton), who was also a magistrate, was concerned with a similar study of the state of knowledge in the field of treatment research and published her analysis in 1959 under the title *Social Science and Social Pathology*(75).

Barbara Wootton's approach was, as she says, essentially practical: "My original interest in the subject matter of this book sprang from practical experience . . . it was the unanswerable questions which forced themselves upon my attention as a magistrate serving both adult and juvenile courts in London . . . while on the other hand eight years as Head of a University Department training students for social work provoked much reflection." Whether one agrees with Professor Wootton's conclusions or not, it must be agreed that her experience is almost unique in this field and qualifies her to speak with authority.

After a very thorough search of the literature, Professor Wootton selected 21 pieces of research in the areas of crime prevention and treatment. Her reasons for rejection of a much later larger body of material are quite sound, even though she excluded many works previously respected in the field. She had certain requirements for each study: that it deal with at least 200 subjects (not, surely, an unreasonable number if any generalizations are sought), that it contain data on not less than half or nearly half of that number (this is a very generous allowance indeed in view of the bias that loss of information for a much smaller percentage could entail), and that the hypotheses under study be sufficiently substantial and include accounts of both the findings and the methods used.

These requirements do not seem unduly severe when it is realized that far more exacting standards are required in almost any acceptable piece of marketing research. Yet, Wootton states:

. . . a few of the better known studies of delinquency had to be omitted on one or more of the following grounds: because they produced insufficient material, because their statistical findings could not be divorced from the text or were presented in a form which defied comparative use, or because the samples used were inadequate. [Thus] Shaw and McKay's famous ecological study and Lander's Baltimore investigation were excluded on the first ground, Stott's work on Delinquency and Human Behavior on the second and Bowlby's celebrated study of affectionless thieves on the third.

From the viewpoint of assessment of treatment outcomes, the majority of those accepted according to Wootton's criteria are no longer admissible today, and many others that have since appeared should also be excluded on the more rigorous expectations of research design. Thus, although she admitted Healy's work, *The Individual Delinquent,* 1915, (35), the 1,000 cases dealt with were those "about whom sufficient data were available," doubtless a highly biased sample.

Despite reference to about 400 articles and books, Wootton concludes that "we have little solid factual evidence." Moreover, many other summary works were considered, and that of M. Metfessel and C. Lovell, 1942 (50), is quoted with approval where they say that "the longest lasting [theories] are those which deal with vague categories . . . [the] more concrete measurable factors which can be more easily put to the test are seen to lose their significance as soon as they are subjected to really vigorous [*sic*—rigorous?] scrutiny."

It is difficult to find any reasonable grounds for disagreement with the conclusion that the major achievement of research in the field of social pathology and treatment has been negative and has resulted in the undermining of nearly all the current mythology regarding the effectiveness of treatment in any form. As Wootton points out, however, this is no excuse for not giving careful consideration to treatment policy.

It is not surprising that Bailey concludes his study of the 100 research reports on the outcome of penal treatment:

If one were to eliminate from the "successful outcome reports" all studies characterized by questionable research methodology and procedures, the percentage of successful outcomes based upon reliable and valid evidence would be small indeed. . . . Perhaps, it is time for correctional treatment personnel to re-evaluate some of their basic assumptions regarding the nature and etiology of delinquent and criminal behavior.

In the years that have passed since Bailey's summary and Wootton's analysis and critical survey of work in this field is there any new development that has more promise?

■ Trend toward rigor and complexity

A distinct trend *can* be noted. At about the time that Bailey and Wootton were reporting the state of ignorance and the sorry situation regarding methodology, a few studies were beginning to appear that showed promise of developing into a reasonable means of evaluating treatment and social action. The trend began with the application of some modification of the prediction methods. Some of the results of this approach raised questions on which there was further enlightenment from some experimental design studies conducted by the U.S. Navy Retraining Command. The relationship between information and decisions was beginning to be noted and utilized. The questions that began to be asked were better questions in that they were more closely related both to the methods available and to the practical aspects of the problems studied. (For a more detailed discussion, see page 150.)

S. Adams, 1967 (1), summarized the outcomes of eleven projects carried out by the California Board of Corrections, five projects by the Los Angeles County Probation Department, three by the California Youth Authority, and three federal probation studies. He noted that in nearly all cases the initial studies revealed no differences between the experimental treatment and the conventional program. Only later studies began to reveal significant programs and significant pay-offs from the innovation. It is perhaps also reasonable to summarize this result by noting that after the initial studies which were "unsuccessful," it was possible to devise more complex models on the basis of the information generated by the earlier research. Thus, it may well be that without the *lack of success* of the earlier studies, there would have been no basis for the later successful studies! There was a tendency in each project to begin testing relatively simple theories, and, perhaps not surprisingly, the simple explanation was shown to be inadequate.

It is perhaps a feature of research workers that they become experts in one area of applied research and enthusiastic about a particular form of analysis, system of experimentation, method of measurement, or type of problem. Give any problem to some psychologists and they will immediately factor analyze it! Suggest some other area to some criminologists and they will set out at once to predict it. Although prediction is a form of classification, those who have followed the prediction interest have failed to take much interest in other forms of classification. Those who are interested in forms of classification have not been particularly interested in prediction or risk categorization.

Only in the most recent work have we found the relationship between risk categorization and other forms of classification of types of offender. In other studies the risk factor was taken care of, to some extent, by randomization of the input to the different treatment systems that formed the demonstration program.

Clearly the more complex the model, the more complex the information necessary to enable control of the model. Early failure to prove what was desired seems to have provided incentives needed to collect more sophisticated information and to spend the necessary funds in the provision of information. A further means whereby information has been brought into line with the situation is by simplification of the problem through increased specification and limitation of the conditions. Initially a common fault had been in attempts to cover the big problems with little information, perhaps because they were considered as "really very simple." The demonstration of complexity with the proof that failure was mainly due to a belief in simple solutions provided information as to how to proceed. Thus, the unsuccessful studies were, perhaps, the more valuable and useful.

In England and Wales, the official research unit began in 1953 with a prediction and evaluation study which seemed to demonstrate the kind of thing that every humanitarian social worker wanted to have "proved"—that treatment in open conditions was superior to treatment in closed conditions. This inference was possible from the study by H. Mannheim and L. T. Wilkins, 1955 (45). There was then a tendency, as expressed by one newspaper, for people to believe that "research workers labor for years . . . they study many figures . . . only to conclude what every reasonable person knew already." Perhaps California was more fortunate in that their early studies were "unsuccessful," tending to throw doubt upon what "everybody knew already."

ATTENDANCE CENTERS STUDY (CAMBRIDGE)

A very interesting result was obtained by F. H. McClintock, M. A. Walker, and N. C. Savill in their study of attendance centers in England, 1961 (46). They calculated two different prediction tables, one of which they termed the "penal score" and the other the "social score." The two scores utilized different items of information, but both provided good discrimination between subsequent successes and failures. The attendance-center sentence is a court order requiring the young offender to spend a given number of hours during weekends at a center that is usually administered by the police department. In addition, some offenders are placed on probation for 1, 2, or 3 years—normally 2 years. McClintock, *et al.,* noted that the offenders who were required to attend the centers and who at the same time were on probation were more often failures than those who were only required to attend the center.

Those who had the double requirement of probation and attendance were, as might be expected, worse risks on the average than the others. However, using the "penal score" they found that after allowance for the class of risk, those who also served probation were still more frequently failures than expected. With the "social score" an exactly similar result was found. Their data are summarized in Table 1.

TABLE 1. *Comparison of offenders not on probation and on probation*

| | PENAL SCORE | | | SOCIAL SCORE | |
| | Percentage of Failure Rates | | | Percentage of Failure Rates | |
Score	No Probation	Probation	Score	No Probation	Probation
1–8	48	62	Under 21	52	61
9–10	41	57			
11–12	35	47	22–25	31	45
13–14	30	37	26+	23	35
15–16	23	35			
Number of cases	632	545	Number of cases	632	545

SOURCE: Adapted from F. H. McClintock, *et al., Attendance Centers* (London: Macmillan, 1961) (46).

The consistent pattern of the results for both types of prediction score and the fact that they are derived from a sample size somewhat larger than has been usual in this field are both very important points. The authors calculated a combined "social and penal prediction score" and again compared the outcomes with the expectation in terms of the calculated risks. The results were exactly similar, the range for probation cases being from 30 percent failure to 61 percent failure, and for the nonprobation cases from 18 percent failure to 55 percent failure. In further support of this evidence it was noted that "the rates of success were fairly high in cases where the attendance-center orders were imposed independently of probation; 75 percent among first offenders and 50 percent among recidivists." Where the attendance-center order was combined with a probation order the success rates were 69 percent for first offenders and 48 percent for recidivists. Thus, even the single piece of information regarding the prior record of the offender gives a result of a similar kind to that obtained by the more complex and powerful prediction scores. The authors of the Cambridge study (46, pages 83–84) do not develop any theories on the basis of these findings, but they provide three suggestions (one as a footnote):

1. Probation is causing the failure rate to increase.
2. Various factors other than those included in the investigation have influenced the magistrate in placing the boy on probation.
3. A conflict between the aims of probation and attendance-center orders may account for this anomaly.

They regard 2 as the "more plausible," and suggest that the "attitude of the offender in court" may be one of the factors related both to selection for probation and to the chances of "failure" under the attendance-center order. Thus, they opt for a "residual information" explanation; other factors were utilized subjectively that were also predictors of failure, and in cases where these applied, the courts tended to award probation as well as make an attendance-center order.

Since the court was not required to make any subjective assessment of likely outcome, it is impossible to test this explanation. In all studies to date there has been a conspicuous failure of subjective prognosis to account for more than a very small proportion of the variance in subsequent behavior. The authors' belief that the subjective utilization of information *additional to that used in the building of the scores* provides the "most plausible" explanation would seem to ascribe almost divine insight to the magistrates concerned. Indeed, the authors (46, page 95), themselves reported that "officers themselves tried to assess or predict the after-conduct of the offenders sent to them by the juvenile court." Such "predictions were successful in 66 percent of the cases . . . no better than if every offender had been indiscriminately classified or 'predicted' as successful." If the subjective assessment of the officers whose task was the treatment of the offender were so notably unsuccessful in "prediction" (although no worse than is usually reported), how can the magistrates be considered so much superior in theirs? It does not appear that the "residual information" explanation is very plausible; rather, the results that show a combination of treatments to be poor treatment might be interpreted on face value. It may be convenient to believe that two obviously good things together must be better than one singly, but the study's evidence is to the contrary.

The first interpretation (1) that "probation is causing the increase in failure" has no support from the data, because the project did not include cases where probation alone was applied. For this explanation to be made even in the most tentative terms, it would seem necessary to have comparisons between cases given (1) probation alone, (2) attendance center alone, (3) attendance center plus probation. The simplest hypothesis that can be put forward as an interpretation of the results is that *the least that it is possible to do with offenders, the better the outcome!* Alternatively, because attendance centers are essentially simple in terms of operation and the requirements made of their attendees, and give little or no attention to therapeutic concepts, the *simpler the setting for treatment,* the better it is for these young offenders. Probation alone is more complex than attendance center alone, and probation plus attendance center is even more complex. This is in accord with the third explanation suggested by the authors; the role expected of the offender by the attendance center authorities is very different from the role expected of him by his probation officer.

The methods used in this study are among the most sophisticated found in the literature to date. A particular note should be taken of the calculation of two styles of prediction tables, the use of these to partial out differences between the risk classes of offenders dealt with in two ways by the courts, and the fact that it was subjected to a validatory test against a different sample of 208 cases. The validation sample continued to show results similar to those quoted above in respect to the attendance-center orders with and without probation, although the over-all failure rate was higher, particularly for the poor risks, in the second sample. The second sample was analyzed to test whether the higher failure rate could have been due to the greater proportion who were also given probation, but this did not appear to be the complete explanation.

Perhaps the study of attendance centers was the first to indicate from a prediction viewpoint the necessity for examination not only of an interaction between the offender and the "treatment," but the possibility of interaction between elements within a treatment that may militate *against* the rehabilitation of the offender.

7

More complex models develop

PREDICTION TOWARD EVALUATION

Obviously, the outcome of any process or treatment is determined in part by the nature of the "input" material. The different outcomes of different forms of treatment can be explained by the difference in the classes of offenders selected by the decisions of the courts. Any comparison of the outcomes of any two or more treatments must make allowances for the nature of the input in order to make necessary compensation.

By definition, presentence estimates of the probability of recidivism give one measure of the type of input material. The development of prediction methods supplies a tool of analysis so that a "base expectancy" can be stated; if differing treatment outcomes result, they would be required to show over and above any such "base" rates. If two populations have the same presentence probability of reconviction, and after treatment the outcomes are found to differ, it might well be assumed that either the different treatments or other concomitant variables may afford some explanation. If no differences appear after adjustment of the observed rates in terms of the expectations, then it would seem reasonable to conclude that there was no difference between the treatments. But it is not all quite as simple as that.

■ *Base rates as control*

One of the first, if not the first, studies to use a variation of prediction methods to assess two different forms of treatment was conducted by H. Mannheim, and L. T. Wilkins in 1953 (45). Initially they used a form of discriminant analysis to predict (estimate) the risk categories for some 700 youths sentenced to borstal training. Borstal training is distinguished from other forms of treatment for young offenders in two ways that concern us in this connection: (1) it is an indeterminate sentence which at that time varied between nine months and three years, and (2) treatment can take place either in open or closed institutions. About one half of the youths were disposed to open institutions after a selection procedure requiring a stay of about four to six weeks at an allocation center. Crude outcome figures revealed that about one in every three of the youths placed in open conditions recidivated, whereas nearly two of every three of the output from the closed institutions were reconvicted within three years.

Using the prediction (estimation) equations, Mannheim and Wilkins were able to show that almost all of the difference between the two types of treatment institutions was due to the differences in the input material. However, there still remained a slight advantage in favor of the open conditions. It was not possible to show whether this was due to the conditions, the superiority of the treatment, the different mixtures of youths (subculture), or possibly other factors. It was clear that the method of "expectancies" provided some means for the extraction of unwanted variation. Later the same basic methods were used in studies by the Department of Corrections and the Youth Authority in both California and Wisconsin and by some other agencies.

Simultaneously and independently, this method was apparently being considered by H. Ashley Weeks (69), who was attempting to evaluate the well-known Highfields Experiment. That a conceptual relationship existed between prediction and the Highfields evaluation is indicated by the fact that the Foreword to

Weeks' book (1958) was written by E. W. Burgess, to whom we have earlier paid credit as a pioneer in the field of criminological prediction.

YOUTHFUL OFFENDERS AT HIGHFIELDS

Ashley Weeks, 1958 (69), attempted to evaluate the new High-fields form of training for younger offenders in comparison with training at the reformatory at Annandale. For various reasons this sophisticated attempt to grapple with the problems of evaluation was not successful, but the reasons were not completely within the control of the research workers. As E. W. Burgess says in his introduction:

. . . a more searching test of the success of the project is the scientific evaluation directed to the questions . . . of comparisons of boys with Highfields experience with boys who have been released during the same period from Annandale Reformatory. The attempt was made, not too successfully as it turned out, to match the two groups in all respects except in the treatment methods of the institutions [69, page xi].

Of course, it is impossible to match on all factors other than treatment, and the method attempted was similar to that used by Mannheim and Wilkins (45).

Some of the questions posed by the Highfields project personnel and, indeed, other project staffs can be answered without difficulty. Such questions as "Is it possible to run an institution of a more relaxed kind without administrative breakdown?" can, for example, be answered by doing it. But the more important questions relate to whether it is worthwhile to do so, and these are much more difficult questions. In this area the answers are usually assumed to be affirmative—if the institution can be run, it must obviously be good.

It seems safe to conclude that Highfields demonstrated fairly clearly and convincingly that money could be saved by the methods employed there, but whether "souls were saved" is doubtful. The Highfields system was cheaper to run than the reformatory system, and there seems little doubt that it was no less effective (or ineffective). In this the results of the Highfields study were in line with other competent research studies that had attempted comparisons of treatments at that time.

The Highfields study is worthy of special note because it represents an honest attempt to answer the important questions of outcome in the light of the material available to the treatment process. In this it has thrown light on other important questions. It is noted, for example, that the "objection can, of course, be raised that the lower rate of recidivism of boys from Highfields is a result not of their experiences there, but of the juvenile courts judges' selection. . . . There is some evidence that the juvenile court judges did, in fact, send boys to Highfields because they thought them better prospects for successful treatment" (69, page xii). Apart from the fact that the design was modified by the judges' actions so that valid inference was prejudiced, there were some further errors. Many of these too may have been outside the control of the research staff. These factors of lack of control prejudicial to the power of inference emphasize the need for a team approach to research planning and operations. With the best of all possible intentions a research design may be damaged beyond repair by the administrative officer, policymaker, or some other person who is not fully briefed on the consequences of any departure from the design.

The particular research workers in the Highfields study were hampered (and they pass over this point all too lightly) by the incompleteness of certain types of information. There was a tendency to make inferences on the basis of information available. For example, the age of onset of criminality is known to be a very important factor in determining the probability of reconviction, yet this was known in respect to more of the Highfields boys than those who were placed in Annandale Reformatory. From other work it is known that the absence of information is itself a factor of considerable significance in assessments of the probability of reconviction. Moreover, it is not known whether the absence of information was correlated with actual information in other sectors.

Prediction equations were worked out only for data on Highfields boys and then applied to Annandale boys. This is altogether unsatisfactory. Any attenuation of the prediction system will be projected as relating to the differences *between* the two groups. If the equations had been applied to another group of Highfields boys, attenuation (shrinkage) would be expected. The nature of the shrinkage may account for the differences that, nonetheless, are reported as demonstrating that "successful boys differ but unsuccessful boys do not." The method of building the equations makes this inference totally unsafe. Under almost any imaginable conditions (and we can only imagine conditions that are not stated), the production of the equation based on the "experimental" boys and then applied to the "control" would load the dice in favor of the experimental group.

There are many technical problems in the use of prediction or other forms of estimation analysis that are built up on the basis of experience of one sample or form of treatment and then used in respect to another form of treatment or a different sample. This is particularly the case where the information differs between the treatments or samples. There can be no way of separating what may be due to the differences in the quality of the information or its availability from "real" differences between the treatments or samples. Indeed, a prediction equation as worked out for one sample is not a prediction equation for that sample, but merely a fitting of certain parameters *to that sample*. Any generalizations or extensions to other samples require a different form of logic.

Nonetheless, the Highfields study deserves special note. It raised problems that are now better understood and provided a base from which other research could be built. But administrative and social-policy problems are more intractable than statistical and inferential problems. Both must be solved before any inquiry of this type can produce evidence that would be acceptable as proof, or even as disproof of hypotheses regarding effects of treatment.

Classification and typology
of offenders

WHAT IS CLASSIFICATION?

"Classification," in common with many other terms in penology, is often used to mean different things. For example, it is now regarded as necessary to separate male from female offenders in institutions, and in most countries some separation in terms of age and criminal record is also regarded as a basic requirement. But "classification" is not the same as separation or distribution of offenders. Classification centers exist mainly to *distribute* offenders to different institutions, and any systems of classification that do not relate to the function of *distribution* would often be regarded as outside the scope of these centers. Of course, persons must first be classified by sex before they can be segregated by sex, but classification does not in itself imply segregation or distribution. Segregation or distribution can take place at random, but random distribution would not qualify as "classification." Persons must be classified by age before distribution into age groups in institutions can take place, but the degree of precision of age classification may not be required for purposes of distribution.

The purposes of classification are, of course, related to some form of action. In some cases classification may serve as an administrative convenience; in others, for treatment purposes. In hospitals male and female patients are separated for administrative purposes, even where the treatment for both sexes may be exactly the same. It is also usually desirable to classify patients by the major divisions of treatment—medical or surgical—and to accommodate each of the two groups in distinct locations. But any one person can be in only one location, while there is no limit to the number of possible classifications. It is unfortunate that classification of offenders has come to be associated with a locational concept; it is a prerequisite of the determination of location but is otherwise independent of it.

All persons or objects may be divided, notionally, into various sets or classifications. All "moving things" belong to a class or set of "moving things." Persons move, unless they are in certain states, and may be said to belong to this class. Indeed, the process of *identification* may be regarded as the determination of some class to which an object belongs, or the determination of whether an object or person belongs to a given set or class. The choice of class depends upon the use to be made of the classification.

DISTINCTION BETWEEN PREDICTION AND TYPOLOGY

Any system of measurement or estimation may, of course, be used for classification. If we measure the weights or heights of offenders in any institution, it is possible to classify them into any number of separate categories or to describe each one uniquely as an individual with a weight or height different from all others. The *function* of classification is the important consideration, not the mere fact of classification or even the type of classification. In some jurisdictions the type of risk—expressed in terms of the likelihood of rehabilitation or recidivism—is taken as a feature of classification. The United States federal system is a notable example of such classification.

In general, when people in the field talk about the classification of offenders, they have in mind something different from the classification according to one particular factor, such as height, weight, or risk category. Two methods of approach to this problem may be distinguished. One seeks to consider classification in terms of possible types of action; the other seeks to relate the classification to the nature of the input information itself. In the former case a classification (unspecified) is sought that will relate to what *ought* to be done about offenders who fall into any of the categories of this idealized classification. Those who are "alike" according to this idea of classification should (The basis of "should" is often in doubt!) be treated more alike than those in other categories. A valid basis for *should* is perhaps the idea that by such differentiation of treatment the desired outcome may be more likely to be achieved than by any other process or by means of any other form of classification.

The other idea of classification is related to forms or factor analysis and similar techniques. In these systems of analysis the internal evidence is examined in its own right instead of referring to operational or action-based concepts. Ways are sought to simplify a mass of information, but with no specific purpose in mind except the simplification. This may be done by reference to the information or to the individual to whom the characteristics (information) apply. In the latter case, a system of classification results because the method requires that persons be placed in groups which are more alike than those placed in other groups. This concept is perhaps best thought of as a kind of "generalized likeness," where the base of reference is the whole set of information collected regarding a sample of persons. There are many varieties of approach to this form of typology.

It will be obvious that prediction methods of classification by risk category do not fit into either of these classes of classification. Knowledge of an individual's prediction score (estimate of the probability of recidivism) does not relate to any *general* idea of "alikeness" to other offenders nor to the concepts that may underlie a treatment program. Prediction methods can claim only to provide an estimate of the expected outcome of treatment (or no treatment) either in general or with specific restrictions. Prediction does not provide a diagnosis, only a prognosis. The analogy with medicine may hold sufficiently well to clarify this point. A prognosis tells that a person has a poor or a good chance of recovery after an operation. This information is usually utilized to provide guidance as to whether the operation should or should not be undertaken; it also provides guidance for decisions by the patient and his relatives as to what might be wise planning in the circumstances. Nonetheless, survival probability estimates (prognosis) provide a means for measuring the effectiveness of treatments of different kinds. But, prediction methods do not normally assist in the discovery of effective means of treatment. With certain other forms of classification there are different expectations. There is no general instrument or form of assessment that can be used for all purposes.

An experimental study may reveal that "bad risks" perform better under one form of treatment than another. Should this be demonstrated as so, it clearly has nothing to do with the simple fact that those involved are "bad risks." Alternatively, it may be shown that while bad risks vary in relation to treatment outcomes in different kinds of treatment systems, good risks show less variation. Again, this could have nothing to do with the class of risk as such.

If there were available two estimates of an individual's probability of recidivism—one, under treatment T1 and another under treatment T2, for example—it might be reasonable to select the treatment associated with the smaller estimate of predicted recidivism. But the estimate of probability itself tells us nothing; it is our comparison of the two from which we infer the rationality of a certain decision.

There is no reason why bad and good risks should not benefit, perhaps equally, from the same treatment. It is, however, very difficult to say exactly what is meant by the word "equally" in this connection. If a bad risk showed an 85 percent probability of recidivism in treatment T1 and 80 percent in treatment T2, while a good risk showed a 15 percent chance in treatment T1 and 10 percent in treatment T2, would this be an "equal" difference? It will be clear that where comparisons are made between treatments and risk categories, a much more complex system of inference is necessary than with single statements.

With classifications of offenders by factors other than the probability of recidivism, the situation might be different and more amenable to development. If something can be said about the type of offender by some classification by factors other than risk, it might be possible to make further inferences. This could be the case irrespective of the basic form of classification, that is, whether it was classification by some concept of a generalized informational distance between groups (using a large amount of interrelated information) or whether it was related to a theory of treatment. The approach from a theory of treatment may seem attractive, but how can a theory of treatment be initiated? Does not the development of a theory need some basis in experience? If so, then should not the rigorous treatment of "experience" in the form of information networks (matrices) be a powerful tool that could stimulate the imagination?

There are, then, different bases for classification. There are those that utilize the estimation of risk; these have appropriate and inappropriate uses. There are those that reduce complexes of information; these have some utility. There are those that simply use information as a means for dividing persons into groups.

Are these distinctions merely academic and therefore of no significance in the task of evaluating treatment? It is claimed that this is an important matter and one of considerable substance, and some empirical evidence may be given in support of this claim. We shall, however, not go into the technical details of the statistical operations, many of which are determined to a greater or lesser degree by the ways in which the data may come in from the field. If we wish to deal with dichotomies, attributes and variables in a combined form, there are requirements that must be met or sets of assumptions that must be made. In some relevant sectors of statistical theory there are many unsolved problems, and it may be necessary to select from a number of forms of approximations. Development of these areas needs the active cooperation of mathematical statisticians working with members of the concerned disciplines.

THE IMPORTANCE OF TYPOLOGICAL CLASSIFICATION

Until recently, it was possible to summarize the results of almost all of the rigorous research studies that have looked into the possibility of differential effects of treatment by saying that once adjustment was made for differences in the input the differences in the output revealed no treatment effect or differential treatment effects. This statement might be taken to mean that there is no generally good treatment, no treatment that is "better" than other forms of treatment for all types of offenders. It became necessary, therefore, to consider a modified hypothesis, that the outcome of treatment can be more effectively examined if an interplay is postulated between types of treatments and offenders. This type of hypothesis permits the expectation that different types of offenders may respond differently to the same treatment, or that a form of treatment which may be indicated for one type of offender may be contraindicated for another type. By this reasoning, the failure to note differences between treatment outcomes in the past could be due to the single form of treatment having differential effects on different types of offenders.

This line of thought owes much to analogies with medical treatment. If delinquency is seen as an "illness," then it is necessary to find the nature of the different types of ailments that have thus far been classified together. If we accept this analogy, it immediately appears that what is effective treatment for one offender is dangerous for another. Two research studies have been noted (see pages 80 & 96) that make this issue more than a probability. Other studies are currently planned that take this type of hypothesis as their central consideration.

■ *Interaction effect demonstrated*

The first study of this kind is believed to be one that was carried out by the U.S. Office of Naval Research under the direction of J. D. Grant (30). Offenders were studied most intensively and classified in many ways, but in particular they were classified according to measurable personality characteristics related to the ways in which they perceived the world, and especially the world of other persons. A scale that gave an indication of the level of "social maturity" was devised and was related to a theory of treatment.

Three different types of treatment were available, and after classification and placement in a pool, individual offenders were allocated to each of these, at random. The experimental design was commendably rigorous. Two treatments made use of intensive "living group therapy"; the other was more similar to the usual form of treatment in a naval corrrectional establishment. The results of the different treatments in the different groups were tested by follow-up, where the criterion of success was a return to satisfactory performance of duty, as assessed by the offender's unit commanding officer.

It is not possible to detail the experiment here. The main importance of the results, however, is not in terms of detail but in their general nature. The results show the percentage success for three experimental treatments and are given in Table 2.

TABLE 2. *Results of Some Experimental Treatments for Nonconformists in the Navy*

Offenders' Personality Type	Treatment Type		
	T1	T2	S
Socially mature	70	72	61
Socially immature	41	55	60
Total sample	59	65	61

SOURCE: J. D. Grant and M. Q. Grant, "A Group Dynamics Approach to the Treatment of Non-Conformists in the Navy," *Annals* (322), 1959.

It will be noted that the row and column summary percentages show no significant differences either between type of treatment or type of offender. Treatments T1, T2, and S have about the same general success rate. But the *interaction* between the type of offender and treatment, T1 especially and to a lesser degree treatment T2, is notable. Treatment S did not, as expected, interact with personality differences. Although treatment T1 was designated the "best" treatment, the socially immature were less likely to benefit from it than from treatment S, while the mature offenders were more likely to show success if subjected to the intensive group therapy (living group) methods.

What exactly "socially mature" might mean and exactly what was the nature of the interaction remain somewhat uncertain. It is, however, quite clear that merely to ask whether a treatment is "good" or "not so good" for offenders is not a meaningful question. Questions must also be asked about the types of offenders for whom any "treatment" is regarded as likely to be "good," where "good" means "effective" in terms of some criterion of success. There is no question here of humanitarian problems. Such problems need consideration, but they are independent of questions of effectiveness. Humanitarian considerations set the boundary conditions of experiment and action, and, although it has been found that humanitarian treatments are *no less* effective than severe and costly forms of treatment or punishment, there is no reason to assume that humanitarian treatments are *necessarily* more likely to pay off in success. Effectiveness is measured by evidence. After such evidence is available, ethical considerations have a sound basis from which to develop.

Following the study by Grant, *et al.* (30), as noted above, other studies have shown features that can only be described as interactions, and these factors seem to be of considerable significance. The interactions are, of course, statistically assessed; they say nothing about the process involved. It is, nonetheless, very clear that something termed "interaction" (and we must use this word until we can describe the process more adequately) takes place. That is to say, we cannot explain the observed outcomes of treatment in terms of a linear relationship between risk category and success rates. Nor can we describe outcomes adequately in terms of types of offenders and types of treatment. Rather an interaction between *types* of treatments and *types* of offenders provides a better explanation of the observed variation in success rates. The study by Grant, *et al.* (30), makes this postulate more convincingly than most others because of the randomization of cases to the various treatments. Moreover, the treatment variants were specified and described in advance of the experimental action. Note, however, that Grant's study did not include the calculation of expected rates of recidivism for different classes of offenders but relied only upon a typology. Randomization would, of course, give the expectation that the mean success rate for each group would be similar, and this, in fact, was observed. But problems arise because randomization creates a situation that cannot be assumed to be totally independent of the treatment effect. (See Chapter 15 for further development of this type of experimental design and for notes on the problems of interpretation of results.)

The study of attendance centers (with side glances at probation) carried out by the Institute of Criminology, Cambridge, England discussed earlier on page 80, included neither randomization nor a typology. Two different equations of risk estimation and a combined form of these equations were calculated. None of these equations fitted the observed rates of recidivism for the different treatment classes with equal precision, and the best explanation, in light of other research, would seem to be that the study demonstrated either (1) an interaction between treatment type and offender type, for which, in the absence of a typology, no assessment was feasible; or (2) an interaction between one treatment and another treatment where two different treatments were combined, a special case in this study. The authors themselves, although noting the possibility of interaction as an explanation, opted for the possibility that the method, together with the court action could have given rise to the observed results.

It seems safe to conclude that there is strong evidence to support the idea of interaction effects; the observations noted in complex studies can the better be explained if such postulates are entertained. If a typology of offenders is not attempted in the research design, there can be no way of testing the postulate that different persons interact differently with different treatments. If estimates of the probability of recidivism (risk factor) are not calculated, it is possible that differences in risk may be confounded with typology. If treatments are not described, the possibility that component parts of the treatment are interacting to the disadvantage of the whole cannot be explored. It is, of course, not possible to explore everything at once, and randomization, although taking care of many factors that cannot be otherwise dealt with, cannot be relied upon to meet all issues.

One thing is clear: The simple "cause-effect" concepts will not suffice. The questions we must ask and the answers we hope to obtain must be more complex than has previously been thought.

CAUSE-EFFECT AND COMPLEX MODELS

Although we cannot be sure even of this, it now seems that a reasonable research strategy would begin to develop models that postulate interaction effects of various kinds. Such effects are of many possible forms, and they can be studied from various viewpoints. In particular, in the preceding discussion, the distinction between the *purpose* of classification and the *methods* of classification should be particularly noted. Of course, purposes and methods are related, but it is possible to consider an interaction between A and B by examining and describing the variations in A and relating these to B; or, alternatively, we may begin by examining and describing B and relating variations in B to A.

Even today in medical science two distinct approaches may be observed. We may begin by first finding a new drug and then posing the question as to what disorders it might most effectively cure or alleviate. There is also the approach from the other end; a disorder is studied, variations of it are isolated (for example, the common cold), and attempts are made to find a suitable treatment. The two different approaches may be equally sound. It is only the end result that describes the pay-off.

Two similar methods of approach are now beginning to emerge in studies of the treatment of offenders. In the past there were a very limited number of "treatments" for offenders, but new treatment methods are now being devised and considered, and sometimes trials of these new forms are related to concepts of suitable types of offenders who are expected to be "able to" benefit. But all too often the new treatment is seen as analogous with a "wonder drug" that will cure all of the ills of criminals of all types. Only after trials, when it is usually found that certain offenders seem to have benefited and others became worse, is a typology attempted a posteriori. Any a posteriori hypothesis has a very high chance of being sustained by the data from which it was derived! It is easy to be wise after the event, but the value of such wisdom is always in doubt.

TYPES OF TYPOLOGY

The field of social work and criminology has tended to rely heavily upon theories of "need." Theories of need are related to theories of deficiencies, and theories of treatment to the making good of perceived deficiencies. Often the nature of the transition from the concept of need to the concept of treatment is not rigorously made, but the method has potential of development. In criminology, however, the needs of the individual may be related to irreversible processes, and the treatment cannot be directly related to the deficiency that is regarded as being associated with the individual's social incompetence.

It is not appropriate here to go into the general theories upon which concepts of needed treatments have been based. Many theories are in opposition to other types of theories, but if any theory can be worked out in terms of a practical consequence of a possible treatment, it may be reasonable to test its application by reference to the outcome.

Such was the case in the work quoted (30). The tests of "social maturity" did distinguish between types of offenders in relation to the outcome of treatment. Why only the "socially mature" responded to the "best" treatment makes an interesting question for further investigation. It seems safe to conclude that "social maturity" provides a useful classification of offenders in relation to attempts to maximize the successful outcome of treatment in institutions. Whether it is the optimum system of classification or not (and it is highly doubtful that it will prove to be the optimum), it clearly has some element within it that merits further work. Perhaps its main problem as a system of typology is that it is complex and almost certainly not unidimensional. (An unpublished factorial analysis [6] seems to demonstrate the multidimensionality of the Grants' scale.)

Not only may some of the classifications used in typological exercises to date be multidimensional, but it seems certain that all forms of "treatment" for offenders are also multidimensional. If this is so, and if complex treatments have elements that interact positively and negatively (see page 80) with the "needs" of the offenders subjected to them to the prejudice of the outcome, some very sophisticated research is still necessary to throw any significant light upon the problem of treatment.

A different approach, and one that is not generally appreciated because it makes use of mathematical methods, is one that starts by attempting a typology of offenders by taxonomic system of analysis. At present this method seems to offer many advantages, particularly as electronic computers can be used to cut the time and cost of heavily detailed arithmetical work. Information is utilized regarding the offender and his offenses, together with any other descriptive material that it is postulated might help to discriminate one offender from another. Different forms of typological investigations have the same end purpose—the identification of a suitable form of treatment for different types of offenders.

Taxonomic analysis provides a simple method of investigation. While it assumes that a pay-off is likely and ultimately to be found in the interaction between the offender and the treatment, it does not start by making statements about these interactions. It begins by assuming that offenders are variable, that there are many ways in

which they vary, and that this variation may be simplified by patterning if the patterns can be discovered. The patterns that can
be identified by the various techniques then provide a means for
considering the variations in treatment, either currently available or possible within the immediately foreseeable future. Instead
of commencing with an idea that "social maturity," for example, is
of significance in the treatment of offenders, we may begin by stating that we want only to find offenders who as a group are as similar
as possible in terms of a large body of information that we think
might be relevant. It may then seem a reasonable strategy to test
hypotheses that the different types of persons thus identified would
profit best if their treatments also were differentiated. We do not
yet know in what ways, but we can focus upon the problem better
because it has been simplified. However, it has not been simplified so much that it has been reduced to hopes about causation or
generally good treatments suitable for all offenders.

Taxonomic classification recently developed by mathematical
botanists has been attempted on a pilot scale in criminological research by P. MacNaughton-Smith and L. T. Wilkins (48). The
botanists were interested in classifications of complex sets of information regarding tracts of land and other features of data. About
any tract of land a large body of data could be collected, and the
question they sought to answer was how different sectors of land
could be described as more similar to, or more different from, other
tracts in terms of the total quality of information. In such cases the
information would relate to the types of plants they observed growing on the particular tracts. In a similar way we may collect a very
large body of information about offenders and then pose the question as to which offenders are more similar or dissimilar and sub-
divide the total into groups where the differences between the
groups are maximized and the differences within the groups minimized. The total quantity of information available can be used as
the basis for determining "likeness." But there are several procedures from which to select, and the choice of method is important in relation to the objectives sought.

It is possible to take the quantity of data regarding a large group
of offenders and to search the whole pattern of associations between items of information with a view to finding the one person
who is the most eccentric, that is, least like any other person in
the group in terms of the total quantity of data. We may then remove the set of data that applies to this person in order to consti-

tute a set of one. We may then search the patterns of information for all persons other than this eccentric to find the person who is most like him, then remove and add him to the set of one. We then have removed the two "most unlike" persons from the group and have a group of two, and a group of the remainder. The total variation within the subdivided groups will be less than the sum of the variation for the whole group before separation of the two eccentrics. The process of identification and transfer can continue until the transfer of any additional person would not reduce the summed variance; at this point a kind of optimal division of the population into two groups has been achieved, because this grouping minimizes the variation within the groups and maximizes the variation between them.

Another method takes the total group of offenders and divides them into two groups according to the particular piece of information which provides the maximum discrimination between them. This process can continue until the significance of any further groupings is too low or the numbers in any one category are too few.

One of the more difficult problems in this type of analysis arises from the fact that there are $2^{n-1} - 1$ different ways of forming groups—an extremely large number of ways with any sample of reasonable size. Rules have to be set up for restricting the consideration of all possible ways for grouping individuals, and within each of these it is also necessary to consider the means for dealing with the criterion factors. Is predictive analysis required or not required? If required, is it desirable to approach it through typology? What are the advantages and disadvantages of different combinations of assumptions and operations in handling data of this kind? It will be some little time before many answers are available to questions of this kind. In addition to approaches like these, there are, of course, the many varieties of factor analysis. The conditions under which factor analysis can provide reasonable material have been hotly debated for years, and the debate may continue for a long while. If used, the methods of factor analysis should, it seems, always be supplemented and compared with as many other methods of analysis as possible.

The various methods of obtaining typological divisions (as distinct from predictive risk divisions) produce data of use in suggesting possible varieties of treatment that may be suitable for the different classes thus identified. If individual offenders, in terms of large quantities of information, tend to divide into certain groups, it may be good strategy to set up and test hypotheses to the effect that the treatments to which they would respond might fit a similar pattern of groups. The quantity of information to be considered is so reduced to that which is of maximum power in discrimination that theory and experience might be more effectively concentrated upon the problems which remain. Another important use of typological analysis is clearly in the examination of the possible different outcomes for different types under different or similar forms of treatment. Typology alone is not a sufficient answer; evaluation and estimation are still required.

Prediction, evaluation, and decision-making

Prediction methods began, as we have noted, with a concern for the decision processes of parole boards; indeed, there was concern from specific parole boards in relation to discharges from particular penal establishments. It was most unfortunate that those involved so quickly departed from this restricted frame of reference which was producing "feedback" information to decision-makers and embarked on attempts at grand theory. Now the focus of attention is again back on the decision-making process. It seems a great pity that this focus was ever lost. How much progress might have been made if it had been retained? Perhaps criminology today would be a leading discipline in the study of decision processes instead of trying to make up for lost time and to learn from those disciplines that moved forward along the decision-study line of inquiry.

It is necessary, for our purposes, to understand the background to the decision approach. We shall attempt a summary here without reference to the underlying mathematical models, and we shall not consider the many forms of development of strategies of the decision process. It is not possible to delve into any consequential issues without coming up against some extremely complex concepts, but the basic ideas are simple.

It will be evident that neither studies of recidivists nor prediction tables provide the types of answers required to evaluate a penal system or even subsystems within a larger system. Even if we can establish the probability of an individual to recidivate, we do not know what next to do to reduce that probability. If we hold that recidivism is directly related to the personality, would we then need to consider changing personality? Because it clearly would be unrealistic to expect all to reform, how much success is to be expected in any such operation? There are other difficulties, as well.

In 1950, the American Psychoanalytic Association set up a committee to "evaluate psychoanalytic therapy." The committee met but reached only one conclusion: that, "in order to evaluate a subject, one must first know of what that subject consists and since apparently no two individuals, not only of the committee, but of the society as a whole, would agree to a definition of psychoanalysis, the committee was at a loss to know how they were to know what they were evaluating" (2). With similar considerations, what is the treatment of offenders? In the institutional setting many experiences will have an impact upon the offender's consciousness. Which of these are treatment and which are operational for the institution? To what extent are routines of training expected to have a transfer value in the learning experience? Is it necessary to be able to answer all these questions in a satisfactory manner before we can discuss evaluation? It depends, naturally enough, on exactly what one means by evaluation and the degree of approximation that one is prepared to accept in any assessments which may be made.

DESCRIPTION IN RELATION TO STRATEGY FOR ACTION

Emphasis in earlier studies in criminology was on the assumed necessity to be able to give precise definitions. The question, "What exactly *is* a recidivist?" seemed very important, whether this question was answered by description or by attempted definition. But we are now more clearly aware of the fact, and its consequences, that the power to make reasonable statements does not depend upon what a thing really *is,* but upon what information we have about it. There is a difference of emphasis here that has a considerable impact upon the strategy of research. The emphasis has moved from a focus upon the person observed (the unique individual) to a focus upon what may be said about him; from a discussion of what really *is* "out there" to a discussion of *what we can say* about what is "out there." What we can say, and not our belief about the "real" thing, is the raw material for logical inference.

The main impact of this transformation of concepts upon research designs and methods of analysis seems to be evident in the emphasis upon interactions. In other words, the early investigators were focusing upon "what was out there," without reference to the viewpoint from which the "out there" was observed. The first thing, they seemed to think, was to establish "truth," and then they would accommodate to it.

NECESSITY FOR COMPARISONS

Today, it would seem to most people a simple self-evident proposition that if we wish to consider the outcome of treatment on offenders, we should be concerned both with the type of treatment and with the type of offender, because the postulated outcome can be seen only in terms of interaction. We no longer affirm that it is possible to find out the truth about the offender, believing that from that truth everything else will become clear. We regard it as likely that the offender may be influenced by his environment and that he himself may be an influence on it. There are no longer any fixed factors; all are variable. We do not seek to establish truth by means of evaluation techniques; we regard it as adequate if we can make reasonable and reasoned comparative statements. As we have noted before, valid inferences can be made only in terms of variation and covariation. The concept of the outcome of a form of treatment has no meaning except in terms of covariation; what has meaning is the *interaction* between the medicine (not its chemical composition) and the disease.

Any inferences regarding covariation must be made in terms of two dimensions independently assessed, namely the treatment and the person to whom it has been administered. A study of *one treat-*

ment, therefore, for what is believed to be one disease, cannot have any logical content. But this was the analogous basis of the studies of recidivists and much criminological work in the past and to a lesser extent continues to be so today. The necessity for controlled variation is now better understood. Nonetheless, some projects, often costing many millions of dollars, are "evaluated" by the single variable approach. Many demonstration projects merely demonstrate that the particular type of treatment was possible without public outcry. (See, for example, the report on the Highfields project, page 88.) The absence of a public outcry is an external factor usually assumed rather than demonstrated in the study itself, but the importance of this *external* piece of information adds something to the logical content of such operations. Usually even this information has to be assumed or, as it were, imported into the reading of the material. Such studies, like works of art, just *are.* It is possible to demonstrate that a thing is possible by doing it and demonstrating that it has been done! But this is not how we wish to proceed. The wish for other types of demonstration leads many people to import further information or assumptions, and by wishful thinking to read into the reports of such projects more than they contain. How much meaning such project reports have, either for writer *or* reader, depends entirely upon the assumptions imported from external sources to the study itself.

Many of the early criminological studies concentrated on demonstrating differences between offenders and nonoffenders, which meant persons in prison and persons not in prison. Apart from the sampling errors noted earlier, it must also be realized that there is no way of identifying the difference between the nontreated nonoffender and the nontreated offender. By definition and process of law, all offenders must be treated; thus, one category contains no observations. There is no way whereby it can reasonably be demonstrated that differences between offenders (treated) and nonoffenders (nontreated) are due to factors other than the treatment itself. To what extent prisoners differ from nonprisoners may be due to the effects of imprisonment—separation from family and the cutting of other communications with the external world. We may think this doubtful, but we cannot demonstrate it either as untrue or even improbable. Should we suppose that the incarceration of an innocent person would have no effect upon his personality as assessed in prison interviews by a person who believed him guilty? Would the standardized questionnaire techniques reveal significant differences, and if so, how would they be interpreted? Almost certainly they would not be interpreted to the effect that an innocent person was in prison. Under these conditions it is impossible to separate the effects of deprivation (treatment) from other traits that may have existed previously.

Nothing should be said in absolute terms about treatment, but it is possible to make comparative statements and to relate these statements to other measures. We may not know what treatment is or what is meant by the phrase "treatment of offenders," but in some sense we have information about it as a concept. We may define the phrase as meaning whatever is done or happens to persons during their period in a penal institution or other penal process. It is not necessarily *we* who are treating *them*; that is a limitation of the concept which cannot be accepted because it is confounded with many other effects. Although we cannot define treatment as to what it *is,* we can, as it were, point to it, and operationally define it as that which happens within the boundary conditions of time and space determined by the decisions of the court. (For example, four years spent in Pentonville, an English security prison in the London area, is a treatment that differs in some respects, known and unknown, from four years in another prison, and both differ rather more from four years on probation.) This form of definition is adequate for communication because other persons are able to understand what we may define by indication. Treatments that may be thus differentiated may be subjected to evaluation in relation to typologies and risk estimates.

NECESSITY FOR VARIETY

We accept that it will never be possible to say what is the "best" treatment, but if there is a variety of treatments available, we should be able to make some statements about our beliefs as to which are in some sense better. Some uncertainty will always remain. What today we may perceive as the "best," viewed from the different perspective of ten years hence we should doubtless regard as by no means ideal. But as we have noted earlier, the "best," like the 'truth,' would seem to imply complete information, and there are good reasons to believe that our information will always be incomplete.

10

Current claims to knowledge

If we are going to get anywhere with evaluation of treatment, we must clearly begin where we now are. Evaluation is a challenge to systems of treatment, but it must itself start from certain assumptions. It is best if these assumptions are as weak as possible in themselves but at the same time firmly established in terms of the information that can be set forth to support them.

In preceding chapters it has been stressed that many assumptions upon which prior research has been based are unsatisfactory and that some of the conclusions reached have been due to the methods employed and not to the phenomena studied. There is much that is unknown, yet there are results of prior studies that seem sufficiently well established to form the basis for additional necessary assumptions for future work.

Many persons would claim more than the knowledge noted in this chapter, and the reader may find a few of the items that were in doubt at the time of publication are now more firmly established. None of the items given as "knowledge" is unassailable;

it can only be asserted that there is a weight of evidence supporting the items claimed, and that because of this support, a longer time will probably have to elapse before these statements will require modification than would be the case for statements based only on individual experience and beliefs.

At present the following claims can be better supported than other relevant claims:

GENERAL POLICY LEVEL

1. Humanitarian systems of treatment (e.g., probation in the community and elsewhere) are *no less* effective in reducing the probability of recidivism than severe forms of punishment. This statement holds with respect to the developed countries of the Western world.

2. Because humanitarian systems usually involve less intervention on the part of the correctional processes, they are normally cheaper than the methods that stress supervision or security.

3. There are many ways in which money (if not souls!) can be saved without having the penal system show any increase in the rate of recidivism.

4. There is no inconsistency between a humanitarian and a cheap and effective system of penal measures, insofar as we have any hard evidence. Harsh measures are supported by the beliefs of many experienced persons, but no known research study has shown any support for these forms of belief.

5. One of the main costs, which from research results cannot be justified, is in the construction and use of unnecessary security provisions. The public pays very heavily for the marginal gains that repressive custodial apparatus and systems may provide. Because the use of "cost-benefit" assessments of effectiveness does not yet present any known situations of conflict with humanitarian principles of treatment, the cost-benefit approach might be extended to cover concepts of public safety and thus provide a measure of the degree of security necessary under certain sets of assumptions.

6. It is generally believed that when an object is defined, the definition (attachment of a label) does not change the thing

so defined. When human beings are defined (classified, and so forth), the act of definition itself modifies the information setting and may thus be said to change the object (person) defined through the definition process. The self-fulfilling prophecy is a factor to be reckoned with in all aspects of criminological and penological decision making for both policy and research.

RESEARCH POLICY

7. Many ways for solving "decision-type" problems are known, but these methods are everywhere underemployed in the penal field. A large proportion of administrative costs are incurred in ascertaining whether public money is being spent under approved budget and accounts headings, but very little is expended in testing whether the money so correctly spent assisted in furthering the *purposes* for which it was provided. It seems reasonable to allot for evaluation studies a proportion of the funds allocated for any operation carried out on behalf of the administration.

8. Evaluation methods are an essential part of any well-run system in providing feedback, whereby the administration is informed regarding the degree of effectiveness with which its intent is being carried out. Evaluation studies are not to be confused with research. Research is needed to establish means whereby evaluation may itself be more effectively (and cheaply) carried out, as well as to establish other results. The distinction that seems operationally useful is in the time focus of the two operations: Evaluation is concerned with assessing what has been done or is currently being done; research is concerned with what might be done and with what the position might be in the future. An analogy with industrial quality control may make this point clearer. Quality control is part of the production process to ensure that the product continues to meet consumer-acceptability standards. Research will be used to establish a quality control system in the first instance, but the operation of the quality control system is not a research operation.

9. Very few if any of the substantive results of criminological

and penological research can be expected to be free from cultural factors. The cultural setting is as important for the consideration of offenders and their treatment as for any other social problems. Methods for solving problems are invariant (or nearly so) with respect to different cultures; hence, a technology of problem solving is exportable. But the solutions obtained in one culture are not necessarily solutions for another culture. It is always risky to assume that "proofs" of any treatment method or any related hypotheses established in one country can be applied with the same effects in another. Pilot trials or other forms of tests are necessary to establish whether the different cultural setting is of significance.

10. Similarly, solutions that may apply at one point in time in any one culture may not continue to apply as technological change induces other changes in the social setting within a country. Sequential test procedures, systems for monitoring the operation of the solutions in practice, and similar research methods must be carefully considered.

TREATMENT

11. No treatment today is standardized, and possibly it never can be completely standardized. There are, in fact, wide variations within any one treatment (as defined by the court disposal) in the operation of the treatment process. It is not even established that variations *within* treatments are less than variations between treatments in terms of the operational variables which affect outcome.

12. There are different kinds of treatments and punishments, both within classifications of disposal and independent of the application of procedures that have been termed "individualization of treatment" within institutions.

13. There are different kinds of offenders and different kinds of crimes. Various means for classification are known, but no means for selecting the best classification is available.

14. Treatment and punishment can be meaningfully considered only as an interaction between types of treatments and types of offenders. Such considerations must refer to typologies.

15. There are, within any institutional setting, forms of "sub-

cultures" that have their own communication networks and norms of behavior.

16. Such subcultures have an impact upon inmates and influence the interactions any single inmate may develop with the form of treatment officially operated. The influence of inmate upon inmate or the inmate culture need not be assumed to be independent of the treatment program; indeed, some systems of treatment attempt to utilize these influences in a positive way.

17. Combinations of different forms of treatment reveal interactions that have been discovered to be negatively related to desired outcome in some specific instances. It therefore seems probable that elements *within* a complex treatment program may also interact, and some of these forms of interaction may be dysfunctional for the treatment programs as a whole. Clearly the assumption that two "good things" when added together into a combined whole are better than either singly is not a sound generalization. Indeed, more of a "good thing" may not necessarily be better than less. More supervision, for example, does not continuously increase the pay-off for all cases; some even seem to be less likely to succeed if given too much help. The degree of "too much" in any instance is not known, but quantitative measures should not be assumed to be linear or additive in terms of each other.

18. Presentence probabilities of individual recidivism can be fairly estimated from information available at that time by use of reproducible and rigorous methods. Such rigorous methods are superior to subjective judgments of probable outcome both as regards the power of the estimation and in terms of methodology.

19. The estimates obtained (as in 18) may be used to describe the types of offenders subjected to different treatments and then to provide a reasonable assessment of their relative effectiveness.

20. Taxonomic classification systems applied to offenders provide a powerful system for subdivision of the total offender population.

11

Setting up an evaluation study

THE MATTER OF CRITERIA

We have defined evaluation as the process of assessing the degree of achievement related to that which has been attempted. What, then, does a penal system seek to achieve? It would appear that the procedures for the disposal of offenders by the courts are intended to achieve not one purpose but several at one and the same time. Unlike those in industry or commerce, penologists refuse to translate their objectives into the dimensions of money. The idea that "cost-benefit analysis" might be used to measure the efficiency of a penal or judicial system has some advocates, but it has far more critics. Again we must ask what the penal system seeks to achieve. It *may* seek to run reasonably quiet institutions where offenders can be kept out of the way for considerable periods of time; it *may* provide some training in certain trades for some offenders but without competing with the scope of legitimate business; and it *may* pursue many other objectives, some of which might qualify to be termed "treatment."

■ *Success and failure*

It seems, however, that the major objective of the penal system (including the treatment aspects) must be to minimize the probability that the offender will recidivate. The early attention given to recidivists lends emphasis to this assumption. No matter what else is done in institutions, and no matter how successfully one may run a prison in other ways, if inmates, after discharge, are found guilty of further offenses and return to custody, then we must regard either the offenders, or their treatment, or both, as failures. An offender enters the penal-system with a particular probability of recidivism; if what happens to him while within the system results in a reduction of this probability, then the treatment has had some success. Similarly, we may say that the treatment which has succeeded best is the one that makes the largest reduction in the probability of recidivism. This is clearly one criterion of a system's success that can be used as a basis for evaluation, but it is not adequate of itself. The considerations necessary in selecting criteria may be illustrated by also noting that the most *certain* reduction in the probability of recidivism is secured by the execution of the death penalty in one form or another!

Another fairly sure way to reduce the probability of recidivism to almost zero would be to keep the offender in a secure establishment for the remainder of his natural life. But this would not be regarded as an acceptable treatment for a petty thief, for example, and the majority of the public would consider this "unjust." However, if there should exist two or more alternatives equally as acceptable to the public as "just," then it might be possible to say that the "best" treatment (among those available and sanctioned as reasonable for this type of offender and this type of offense) was that which reduced the probability of recidivism by the greatest amount. Thus, we might invoke a concept of "room for maneuver" in the decision process. Certain possible decisions (such as death or secure conditions for life) might be inhibited on moral grounds, but other decisions might all lie within the range of acceptable values.

■   *The best—always!*

The phrase "lie within the range of acceptable values" is an important one. Ethics and science come very close together in criminology, yet it is in this field that the boundary conditions are seldom considered in any satisfactory terms. While there is talk of the need for evaluation of treatment, situations are created that prevent setting up any methods for evaluation. Experimental designs are rejected as unethical, because it is considered essential to do the "best," or, "what is needed" in each single case. Thus, while evaluation is asked for, the assumption is made that it is really unnecessary because what is best or necessary is already known. What is "best" or "needed" is that which is selected to be done by those having sufficient power to see that their wishes are carried out. It is seldom conceded that there is a sufficient range of uncertainty to permit random allocation, as in medical clinical trials, where experimentation with human subjects is fully accepted as necessary and ethical.

There are two major and most intractable problems in setting out to consider any evaluation study—the establishment of the aims and the identification of an area of uncertainty where evaluation may be permitted.

Criteria and the room for maneuver are related concepts in connection with evaluation. The objective and the action are here conceptually separated. It is not adequate to say that the judge's intention in disposing of the offender is to commit him to prison, but it is also necessary to say what the intent of *this* action is. At the same time it is necessary to believe in the possibility that the objective might have been achieved by some form of disposition other than that actually given. If there is no permissible variation, the result is the same as saying that the intent and the action taken were totally identical—the action had no purpose other than that within itself. In this case the action cannot be evaluated—if it happened, it was its own justification. This is analogous with some so-called evaluation studies of social-action programs: They were demonstrated to be feasible; they happened, and that is sufficient.

■   *The best intent—always!*

At a slightly different level, the concept of evaluation goes a little further and postulates that although the best was intended by the decision, and, indeed, would have been accomplished if the action had been put into effect in every way as had been intended, for a variety of reasons the actual operation of the action was not carried out in an ideal manner. In such cases the objective of evaluation is seen to be the identification of those practical situations that inhibited the full realization of the intent. This form of evaluation postulates that the decision-makers made the right decisions but that the fault lay elsewhere in the system. While it is possible that the intent of any decision may not be realized, it does not necessarily follow that for this reason the scheme was defective. The divergence from the perceived initial intent might be either an improvement or a deficiency, but which of the two it is must remain an open question in any rational evaluation study.

There is at times a similarity between evaluation that begins with the assumption in the preceding paragraph and general evaluation. The difference depends upon how the intent is expressed. If a person believes that all violent offenders should be flogged and if the flogging is carried out in a manner that bears a close similarity to the way in which it is perceived, the intent (to flog) has been met by the action. We might have to ask whether the intent was to draw blood or to flog without a break of the skin, or we might ask what other perceptions were implied in the "intent."

Would an evaluation of flogging of offenders be adequately carried out if the report provided details of the operation of the action and related these details to the perception of what was likely to happen when the person responsible for the decision made the appropriate order? In this case the answer would almost certainly be "no." But the nature of the example is not a point in the validity of the argument. For example, if we were to replace flogging with vocational training in penal establishments, we might have to ask whether it was intended that *training* be given in an occupation or that the occupation be *learned,* whether it was hoped that when released the offender would follow that occupation for a period of time, or whether it was assumed that such training would result in making the person a useful member of society, and so on. Evaluation, in its full meaning, takes us back to a consideration of first principles.

■ *Law and social protection*

The approach to the problem of the criteria from first principles is difficult. Society has used the prison and its earlier forms of separation from society for centuries, yet no one has explicitly stated the purposes for which the penal system is used, except in very broad generalizations. The principles of protection of society, reform of the offender, and deterrence of others—are said to be combined in the action taken by the court. Yet, the sentence given for similar offenses varies widely and seems to indicate that there is little agreement as to how the principles should be applied.

If the principles are agreed upon and if these principles provide specific guidance to decisions, we might expect rather little variation in the decisions taken. Differences in the types of decisions may of course be due not to differences with regard to the principles but to methods whereby the different principles are to be weighted in any one case. To what extent should deterrence take precedence over treatment, or treatment over the protection of society? Within the three broad principles there is much room for maneuver. How, then, can we begin to set up rigorous criteria?

Despite the wide variation in practice in the nature of the courts' disposals of offenders each jurisdiction has some form of coded law or established a precedent for its own variety of social ethic. In most jurisdictions the legislature has laid down restrictions on the ranges of decisions that the courts may make in disposing of offenders who fall into categories determined by statute. Society is affected by crime, and society has laid down boundary conditions for its courts and penal establishments. Every offender who is found guilty is required to receive some form of punishment–treatment.

MATCHING SITUATIONS

Evaluation of treatment–punishment systems can take place only within this societal setting, and the methods used must be appropriate to such conditions. This means that research methods for evaluation cannot be copied from situations where conditions of this type do not apply. The methods of the physical sciences are not appropriate to social analyses. The situation in which the individual finds himself is an important factor in social behavior that is far too complex to standardize or match in any simple experimental and control design. It is not possible for the research worker to postulate some ideal or some ultimate aim for the treatment process against which he may propose to test an observed situation. The boundary conditions are set by society through the means it has laid down for due process. The research worker cannot attack this system nor seek to circumvent its operation. But variation exists within the system of justice; the boundary conditions are neither rigidly held nor constantly interpreted. The natural variation in the system can be used to explore and evaluate the differences that are permissible, even if not desirable, and that exist within the practical operation of dispensing criminal justice. With cooperation among the several interests in the process of disposition, research designs of considerable power can be obtained.

It is possible that different criteria may not point to the same kinds of action. The protection of society may suggest that offenders should be incarcerated for very long periods of time. But this might be a superficial interpretation of the phrase "protection of society." Incarceration of offenders for long periods is not without considerable cost to the taxpayers, who may regard the cost as a form of overinsurance for the probable risk of further loss, damage, or injury. Thus, even on these grounds, we are back at some concept of probability estimation. It is much more difficult to quantify the concept of deterrence at our present state of knowledge (see Appendix A) and this will not be further discussed here.

GENERAL FACTORS OF SUCCESS

Within the desirable outcomes that relate to reducing the probability of recidivism, there are, however, other considerations. Perhaps an ex-offender may avoid further crimes of theft and instead learn to live on unemployment-insurance payments or on other welfare services. There are many ways in which an ex-offender may fail to become a valuable member of society, and it may be that some small degree of recidivism, if linked with an otherwise productive life, might be preferable to a parasitic existence just within the confines of the law.

Empirical research in England has made at least one useful finding in this area. It was shown that there was a high correlation between the several possible criteria of success of offenders given a form of treatment known as "borstal training" (45). It appeared that no matter which of the criteria had been selected as the one that should be maximized, the results would have been essentially similar. The criteria thus associated with each other were:

1. Subsequent offense recorded against offender (other than a very minor charge dealt with by a fine)
2. Number of subsequent offenses where more than one was committed within the follow-up period of three years
3. Stability of work record after discharge
4. Seriousness of any subsequent offenses
5. Early commission of any subsequent offense after discharge

It is possible that still other criteria might be highly correlated with each other. There would appear to be a "general factor" in relation to the criteria of subsequent success.

It is known that offenders who commit crimes of violence are less likely to recidivate than thieves and other offenders. Yet it is believed that there is a public demand for violent offenders to be punished more severely and for them to be treated as though they were bad risks as recidivists. This kind of result has been found in several countries, but notably in the United Kingdom and the United States (see pages 64–65). The demand seems to be that violent offenders should be dealt with *as though* they were high risks, whereas, in fact, they have been shown to be low risks!

Some of the problems that arise under the heading of criteria of success may best be discussed by specific examples and in relation to various types of projects. Other aspects of these problems cannot be solved without more dialogue between those concerned with social policy and those involved in social research.

■ *Public opinion*

In some types of problems it is possible only to infer the nature of the pay-off (criterion) desired by studying the decision process in operation. This is done by relating the information utilized to the decision process. It may be that persons are behaving in relation to the information available and their room for maneuver as though they were seeking to maximize some pay-off which they cannot make explicit. Their decisions are determined by an intuitive feel of the situation, and their actions reflect some aspect of those whom they feel they represent. Mr. Justice Devlin has said, for example, that if one of his decisions was such that everybody in the court's public gallery was thereby disturbed, he would himself have doubts about its correctness.

In the case of violent offenders who appear before parole boards, it is known that the boards' decisions are determined by factors other than the likelihood of recidivism. Although all prediction tables that have taken account of the factor have consistently shown that the violent offender is a relatively good risk in terms of recidivism, yet parole boards will be more reluctant to release such persons than similar nonviolent offenders with higher risk factors. The decision to release on parole cannot, therefore, be a direct function of the risk of recidivism. It may be that some simple conversion of the simple risk probability could suffice to explain the general nature of the decisions, such as, for example, the multiplication of the risk estimate by some factor that relates to the type of crime for which the offender was first incarcerated. This would be a similar operation to the weighting of risk used in industrial quality control—a producer's risk and a customer's risk. The parole board's (decision-maker–producer's) risk would require larger odds in its favor in the case of certain types of offenses, because, should the offender in fact commit a further crime, the publicity attending the case would reflect adversely upon the board.

Is there any reason why the probability of adverse publicity for the board's decisions should not be employed as the criterion instead of the probability of the offender to recidivate? Such a criterion of pay-off (minimizing bad publicity) would not necessarily be unethical. If the press reflects public opinion and if public opinon is the factor to be considered in the decision process, then it could be a relatively simple matter to quantify this criterion. But there are other methods that rely upon different premises regarding the desired outcome from various decisions in the treatment-punishment process.

It can be said here only that it is necessary to establish some criteria of desired outcome as a basis for evaluation and that research methods can be applied to this kind of problem as well as

to evaluation itself (see, for example, 75). Once the objective of
the system has been described, it is possible to go further in considering appropriate means for evaluation.

■ *Experiments*

There are two different types of approach. The first relies upon
the principles of experimentation, and the second, upon the methods of model building. If it were possible to set up experimental
treatment programs, the problem of evaluation would not arise!
An experimental design is constructed with the purpose of evaluation specifically in mind! The word "experimental" has, however, fallen into rather varied use. In some quarters today it means
no more than an uncontrolled attempt at something new—an administrative innovation, but innovation is *not* experiment. In the
social sciences it is very difficult to set up experiments that meet
the conditions of design (see, for example, R. A. Fisher, *Design
of Experiments* [20].) In any experimental design there must be
an element of randomization. No completely purposeful selection of cases or treatments can provide sound results. In the disposal of offenders the idea that any should be allocated to different treatment–punishment by the throw of a die is generally regarded as a system not commensurable with the concept of justice.
Experimental designs are thus rarely to be found (although there
are one or two notable exceptions in current research). We shall
return to discuss variation of designs that involve some aspect of
random allocation after we have discussed the alternative method
of models.

However, before either of these methods is treated in any detail, there are some elements common to both forms of design that
are of considerable importance. The power of any method of investigation is dependent upon the nature and quality of the information, but in the use of models there are some more rigorous
requirements because we cannot here rely upon randomization
to take care of unknown factors. We shall not stress the necessary
conditions for obtaining sound data but assume that they are understood.

■ *Spontaneous recovery*

H. Eysenck, 1952 (19), made an extensive study of the literature
reporting the outcome of psychotherapeutic treatments for mental

patients. He concluded, as had P. G. Denker in 1937 (17), that roughly two out of every three cases treated showed an improvement or cure. This may seem remarkably good. But he also showed that of those who were untreated, two out of every three recovered spontaneously! (It has been said of the common cold that with treatment it lasts a week and without treatment, seven days!) There is no way of knowing how many offenders would cease to offend if nothing were done about them. We cannot treat them by placebo because they have done wrong. Our action in all cases is confounded with their ailment. In some more recent studies it has been possible to do next to nothing in the treatment of some offenders by placing them on 300-man caseloads and requiring the probation officer to take action only if specifically requested by the probationer. The outcome of cases so placed—and this was a random sample—was no different from that obtained with normal or very small caseloads.

Evaluation of action should, if possible, be compared with outcome of *inaction*. Is it not possible that more careful inactivity might be better than intensive intervention in some kinds of cases?

REGRESSION TOWARD THE MEAN

The phenomenon of spontaneous recovery is much simpler to appreciate than the statistical fact of regression toward the mean. In effect, the results are somewhat similar. If a sample of persons or events is selected or self-selected by some process such that they are not representative of the whole population, then during an interval of time a regression toward the mean will take place such that assessed at a different time, they will be more like the population from which they were selected in the first instance. Suppose, for example, that the number of accidents sustained by persons during a period (t_1 to t_2) were to be noted. Some of these persons, by reason of their accident record, could be identified as "accident prone," which is to say that they sustained many more accidents within the period than was expected. If nothing is done to these persons and their accident record is examined at a later period (t_2 to t_3), the majority will have "considerably improved" due to the influence of chance factors alone. Other persons from the population will have taken their place at the tail end of the accident frequency distribution and will be having their period of bad luck at that time. Only very few will have outstandingly bad luck within two time periods. Among those who appear twice with a high accident experience may be some who are "genuinely" accident prone. But even with accident records the assessment of improvement or deterioration in performance is not easily determined. No general indication can be given as to when this problem of regression toward the mean may be applicable in research designs; rather, all designs must be considered with this factor in mind. Sometimes it appears in subtle ways that are difficult to recognize. The answer is that one must always be on the alert.

12

The inevitability of error

No research result is free from error. No decisions, whether made on the basis of research or not, will always be correct. As briefly noted earlier, the impact of the types of error which occur in all forms of decisions is of two kinds. There will always be some cases where we have acted (decided) as though the person would recidivate, but he does not, and some cases where we have acted as though the person would not recidivate, but he does. In all kinds of decisions we can make errors in one of two ways:

1. Rejecting the hypothesis when it is in fact true
2. Accepting the hypothesis when it is in fact false

Most earlier studies have not recognized one or the other of these, and those that have recognized the types of error have tried to deal with the problem by minimizing the number of errors of either kind. Such a decision is implicit in the statistical measures used. Consider for example Table 3.

TABLE 3. *Types of Prediction and Outcome*

Predicted Outcome	Outcome		Total
	Delinquent	Nondelinquent	
Delinquent	R_1	W_1	$R_1 + W_1$
Nondelinquent	W_2	R_2	$R_2 + W_2$

SOURCE: Compiled by the author.

The cells in the main diagonal are the "correct" prediction entries, and since only numbers (not weights or values) are placed in these cells, the number of units in the other cells are those which are "wrong." But both cells W_1 and W_2 have the same kinds of numbers, and hence any individual who could be removed from one of these cells and recorded in either R_1 or R_2 would represent a gain in terms of the number of persons correctly "predicted." Predictors have preferred the solutions that maximized the number of persons "correctly" classified.

VALUES OF ERRORS

In any reasonable decision-making situation, however, it is unlikely that the two types of error will have identical and equal effect. It may be a far more serious consideration to treat a person who did not in fact later become a recidivist as though he were expected to be one than to treat a person who did in fact later become a recidivist as though he would not become one. Exact ways in which the two kinds of errors differ in consequences do not seem to have been discussed either by those who propose "prediction methods" or by those who oppose them. Perhaps the reason is that these types of error, although common to both subjective assessments and statistical evaluation methods, are brought to light only through the consideration of the statistical approach. Modified forms of the moral-value problems of criteria rearise in the types of errors that can be tolerated. It is of course possible to consider a penalty or negative pay-off associated with every wrong decision and to weight the two types of possible error differently.

If the nature of the criteria are transformed, there are still errors of the same kinds; failure to recognize the two types does not make either type go away. It is interesting that there has been so little discussion of this problem in criminological literature. There is much discussion of decisions in the form of court orders, case work, and the like, but the emphasis is on getting the decisions correct rather than accommodating uncertainty and probability of incorrect decisions. In business the two types of error have been recognized and taken into account because errors of one kind may damage the customer (he may be sold an item that should have been rejected), and errors of the other kind may damage the producer (he destroys an item that in fact was up to standard). Thus, there is a producer risk and a consumer risk and both have to be accommodated. Often the probabilities associated with these risks form the basis of negotiation between the parties.

The decisions made in regard to offenders are, perhaps, more complex than those of business, but the type and nature of the questions relevant to the methods of evaluation are strikingly similar. No matter what decisions are made, no matter how experienced the decision maker, no matter how effective the methods upon which reliance is placed, some decisions will be made incorrectly. (It was, it seems, the realization that an innocent man had been judged guilty of murder that had a considerable influence in the decision of the British Parliament to abolish the death penalty for a trial period of five years.)

PROBABILITY OF TYPES OF ERROR

If it is accepted that wrong decisions will be made from time to time, then it is reasonable to go on to consider what types of error will be made, with what probability, and with what impact. It is not adequate to spend all available resources merely in trying to make all decisions "correct." There seems to be a widely accepted moral code that errors in decisions are of no significance as long as the individual concerned was honest and tried his best to make the right decision. This is neither a moral nor a rational viewpoint. It elevates the belief in perfection or the pursuit of perfection as a goal to an ultimate value; it does not seek to come to terms with uncertainty and the probability of error; it is so obviously unrealistic as to be immoral. The types of decisions most likely to be wrong may not be of as great a significance as those that are less frequently wrong but that have more serious consequences. In other words, some errors are more acceptable than others in terms of some criterion of value. The criterion selected in respect to the assessment of the impact of types of error should be closely related to the criteria selected in relation to the objectives of the system as a total system. The error system is, as it were, a subsystem of the total decision-making system and an integral part of it.

That error is an integral part of measurement appears to be a difficult concept for some persons to accept. For example, critics of the prediction tables point out that in the best risk category, where the probability of success is estimated at 90 percent, there are ten individuals in every one hundred for whom this prediction is "wrong." In one sense this may be a fair statement, although it depends not upon the statement of probability but upon the decision that may be taken in association with that statement. The fact that roughly ten out of every one hundred do not in fact succeed proves that the estimate of 90 percent is *correct*—not that the estimate is wrong in any way. If all of the group succeeded, then the probability would be greater than 90 percent, which is not the case under discussion. The objection has some point if all cases falling into the *90 percent probability* of success class are treated *as though there were 100 percent* chance of success. The failure to accommodate uncertainty is again evident in this kind of argument. The problem of error in this example may be compared with the equally realistic case where the 90 percent probability refers to failure rather than to success of treatment. If all persons having a probability of 90 percent chance of recidivism were treated as though they were all 100 percent recidivists, would this error in any sense be worse than the previous error?

SUBJECTIVE SUPPLEMENTATION

It is sometimes claimed that subjective judgment can help in regard to these kinds of error. Where the tables may fail to find the ten who will succeed in the 90 percent failure group, the human intelligence will be able to identify them. This is sometimes claimed by those who recognize that the human subjective intelligence is not adequate in any other part of the range of assessment. They want to cooperate with the tables, helping them when they fail. These kinds of claims for clinical supplementation of statistical tables have not been supported by any evidence. Their belief that something of this kind of supplementation *should* be possible seems again to originate in an inability to come to terms with uncertainty. For them, probability must be supplemented so that a deterministic model is provided—then a decision can be made!

A probabilistic model, however, is a model in its own right and an appropriate model for decisions under conditions of uncertainty. It does not have to be turned into a deterministic model at the last stage! If decisions are made in the real world, under conditions of uncertainty, the model employed to facilitate the solution of problems in such a world might be expected to be more suitable and powerful if it too were designed to accommodate uncertainty by means of probability estimates. An attempt to change the model from a probabilistic model to a deterministic model by modification of the probability estimates (through subjective assessment) would normally be expected to result in less powerful discrimination. Much more could be said on this and related points concerning the interaction between subjective intelligence with clinical judgment on the one hand, and model building and operational research on the other. There are areas of cooperation that could be developed, but we must limit further philosophical discussion here and emphasize the practical issues of evaluation methods.

13

Operational evaluation

Experimentation that involves some basis in random allocation
to various treatments is often regarded as impossible. The social
administrator refers to his own experience in the field, relates his
experience to that of others and considers that information of this
kind should be capable of use for assessment without all the rigor
of a design. Operational research designs are of this kind.

The attractiveness of base-expectancy methods in evaluation
lies in its independence of administrative or operational processes.
The program may be designed in any way, offenders allocated by
any procedure believed to be good, and yet some form of evaluation may still be possible. No matter what system of evaluation is
used, it is useless unless the operations studied are constant over
the period. Nothing can be evaluated by any means if it is continuously changing; nobody knows what it is and cannot even point
to it because it moves so rapidly!

The power of any method depends upon information collected
and the assumptions which underlie the method of analysis. The

nature of the assumptions that must be made depends upon the method of information-handling selected. We may consider that we select our assumptions and by doing so have restricted our choice of valid methods, or we may first select our methods and thus be forced to make certain assumptions.

A large number of statistical methods are available for the production of "experience tables," "base-expectancy scores," "prediction tables," or other names by which the family of estimates of probabilities may be known. There have been arguments regarding the many and various systems of weighting items that are used in the tables; although some of the arguments have been regarding matters which were not arguable, there are valid points of difference between workers in this area. Currently F. Baker (5) is carrying out an empirical study of a variety of systems using a common set of data, but the results of this work are not available at this time. The arguments do not all depend upon statistical or technical matters related to the solving of equations. Some of the points of difference relate to the meaning of various solutions that, from the statistical viewpoint, may all be equally good.

Before some of these points may be dealt with, it may be necessary for the "users" of the methods to consider the relationship between the assumptions and the types of solutions obtained and the utility of different kinds of solutions. To facilitate such dialogue the following relates the idea of "experience" as usually understood to the idea of "experience tables" and similar methods.

ACTION AND ASSUMPTION

The layman does not usually refer to "experience" unless it is in relation to something else. He supports his arguments or his decisions by invoking experience. The existence of experience *in vacuo* is not a concept that forces itself upon the average citizen. When we begin to apply statistical methods, however, the tabulated experience exists without reference to the decision process. Experience tables merely summarize experience insofar as it concerns recidivism or other phenomena upon which the method of analysis was focused.

If we could know exactly the probability of an individual offender to recidivate, this information in its own right would not tell us what to do. It now seems that earlier statisticians assumed that if people only had a measurement of the situation they would do something about it. It also seems to have been assumed in the field of criminology that if an instrument of prognosis could be made, the action necessary would be simply deduced. In general, it has been thought that offenders who were shown by prediction tables to have a high probability of recidivism *needed further treatment*. Thus, assumptions were made about those very qualities that we are concerned with assessing in evaluation research. But we now know that we cannot take it for granted that longer training would reduce the offender's risk of committing further crimes. It is more reasonable to assume that the longer an offender is kept in secure custody, the longer society is protected from anything he might do. However, the duration of such detention is not the only factor in public safety. If a prisoner is to be released at some time, then the probability of his committing further offenses must be taken into account conjointly with the duration of secure custody. It is possible that the increase in the duration of detention could increase the probability of further offenses and thus more than offset the increased public protection afforded by the time factor alone.

Some assumptions must be made in all kinds of research and social action, but we must intelligently select the assumptions from among those areas which seem intractable because of the nature of the social structure. Social scientists as well as social workers and policymakers are together embedded within the social system. The nature of the assumptions from which we select those we are prepared to adopt and those we challenge in research projects depends upon the variety of the system and the available information.

EXPERIENCE AND "EXPERIENCE"

Experience gained in the course of living differs in one or two important ways from the "experience" to which we refer in the experience tables used in evaluation research. Subjective experience is multidimensional, whereas the experience of prediction tables and the like is unidimensional. That is to say, the normal behavior of the human in gaining experience is through distributed rather than focused attention. No one can stop from noting a person's skin color while measuring his height. The information obtained from records or information as it is utilized in any of the formal systems of analysis need not include a person's color unless this is deemed to be relevant. The human assessor is bombarded with both information and noise. Some information may be relevant to some aspects of his concern, others, to other aspects, but it is received together through the same medium and often simultaneously. The human assessor finds it difficult to distinguish "noise" from "information" in the process of obtaining experience of persons or situations. For the human this distribution of attention is most functional; indeed, it is very doubtful if mankind could have survived without this characteristic. If, while he was working on a cave wall painting, he did not hear the prowling of a wild beast, he could not have hoped to finish the painting! The fact that he was distracted by noise was functional and is still functional today. For some types of problem solving the human intelligence is superior to any computerized analysis, but only for certain types of problems. It is not the method of problem solving that is important, but the method in relation to the type of problem. If we wish to solve problems regarding the treatment of offenders, it is not the means used to obtain a solution we can question, but the power of the answers we may obtain. If better answers are forthcoming from the adoption of computerized analysis, we could not claim to be reasonable men if we did not seek to use this means. Similarly, if the human intuitive (clinical) assessment proves better, we should continue to use and refine these methods of problem solving. We shall need, in either event, to be able to say something about our ideas of what we mean by "better," and once again we are confronted with a problem of criteria or purpose.

The evidence is clear; the human subjective assessment is not reliable as an estimator of probabilities of reconviction as are methods of rigorous analysis by means of models. In some empirical investigations, as has been shown by P. Meehl (49), even really poor statistical models prove superior to clinical judgment. We may say that it has been demonstrated that the processing of information is better done by symbolic manipulation, while the collection of data requires great care and the best attention of the human intelligence.

RATIONAL DECISIONS

In the preceding paragraphs of this chapter and by various inferences in the earlier chapters, three basic concepts have been superficially introduced. We shall now try to systematize them and to expand the arguments, thereby indicating the general forms of methodology which may be applied in operational evaluation that uses prediction and related methods of analysis. The types of information needed for evaluation seem to be classifiable under these three headings:

1. Information regarding the material (input) to be dealt with by the system of treatment
2. The variety of systems available—possible alternative decisions regarding treatment
3. Information regarding the purpose of the system and subsystems involved, or what it is desired to minimize or maximize (pay-off)

Let us refer to these three categories briefly as (1) information, (2) decision variety, (3) pay-off or purpose (criterion). Now if nothing whatever is known (a situation that is difficult to imagine), then there is no point in further consideration; we may as well use the pin as a selection system. We may say that if set (1) is zero, no meaning can be extracted from the system. Similarly, if only one thing can be done—there is no decision variety possible—then here too we cannot make any headway. It should, however, be noted that the decision to do nothing (or by default, in fact, to do nothing) provides an alternative to *something*. When that something is only one thing, we can still stop doing it; and this will provide decision variety. If we do not know what we wish to achieve, then anything we do may be appropriate or inappropriate, and we can subsequently argue that the results which took place were those desired. This kind of rational approach can be reduced to absurdity by any one of the following: We have no information; there is no room for maneuver in the decisions available; we do not know what we want to achieve or cannot state it in useful form.

In the light of this approach we may define one of the goals of evaluation as the discovery of that decision which, in light of the available information, maximizes the probability of obtaining the pay-off desired.

SIMULATION

In some cases it may be necessary for the decision variety to be present in the actual situation under study, that is, in the "real life" situation. But this is not always the case. It is often possible to obtain estimates of likely pay-off from the selection of alternatives where the situation does not exist in fact but is simulated in some way. From simulation it may be possible to select one or two strategies for change that are both acceptable and seem (from the results of simulation studies) to have a high probability of success. Simulation may also be useful in suggesting that the feared results from intervention in the real-life situation may be unrealistic. In Chapter 14 we shall consider how this may come about. A basic concept is the special one of information and its use—the content of the first set noted above.

14

Information and its use

Information is that which reduces uncertainty. It is not all the collections of statements that could be made about a situation or person, because many of these statements might not reduce any uncertainty with which we were concerned. Every item of information that *is* information, as we propose to use the term, tells us something that enables us to do or decide something, without which we could not so do or decide.

That knowledge is partial may seem such an obvious fact as to be absurd to state it here. But correctional workers and even some who would regard themselves as social scientists in the penal field are often, it seems, able to compartmentalize their thinking so that they can agree with this statement but behave as though it were not so. How often does one hear the statement that a little knowledge (originally "learning") is a dangerous thing? If this is true, then it can also be true that a *lot* of learning is a *more* dangerous thing! Unless by "learning" the saying relates to something quite different from "information."

■ *Incomplete information*

It is interesting to note that some persons can reject the idea that decisions are made, without exception, on partial information. Even when one individual decision maker has all the information *he personally* seeks, it is possible to find another individual who would regard a proportion of the information, highly regarded by the first, as irrelevant (as redundancy or noise) and would himself desire to have other and different information.

Decisions are made about offenders, and all these decisions are in terms of partial information. Information is not only less than complete in all cases, but it also has various boundary conditions that are set subjectively in terms of the beliefs of those who have the power to request it. Information also has a cost. It is implicitly or explicitly asked about each item: "Is it worth collecting this item of information?" Thus we can say that information has both a cost and a utility, and we recognize this in our behavior.

COST AND VALUE OF INFORMATION

It is easy to see that information has a cost because manpower is needed to collect and record it, and it occupies valuable space when stored. The costing of information is a straightforward accountancy function. But what of the measurement of utility?

The assessment of the utility of information may be approached through answers to questions of the following type. "What does the knowledge of fact x make it possible to do or decide that would be impossible or impracticable to do without knowledge of x?" This is a sensible question irrespective of the nature of the information (x) or the situation. It may, of course, be difficult to answer this form of question in operational terms; nonetheless, it provides a means for assessing the utility of information (x). We shall discuss how the measurement of value in these terms may proceed, but first, let us extend the concept of utility a little further along these lines. If decisions made without the knowledge of x are exactly similar to decisions made *with* the knowledge of x, then x may be considered to have no utility. In such circumstances it is simpler to regard x as failing to qualify to be called information. It may be redundancy or noise. In such cases it is probable that the addition of x to records may lead to inefficiency. Decisions may be expected to deteriorate if information of no utility is added to existing sets of information.

Information that has a utility assessed by its power as a single item, when added to other information, may increase the total potential power of the set. It does not follow, however, that decisions which are made after reference to the more complete sets of information are necessarily better decisions. It is possible for decision makers to suffer from information overload. The assessment of the utility of information as separate items does not provide adequate assessment for complex sets of information, nor does this assessment give any indication of the methods whereby complex information sets may be used in the decision process.

In this discussion we are not concerned with "false information" or with information that "serves only to satisfy idle curiosity" (whatever that might be). By definition the task of an organization is to carry out what it is designed to do, and for this purpose it requires information. Information that is unrelated to the task is not regarded as information. But let us turn to a further if somewhat different point. So far we have indicated conditions under which x may be said to have zero informational value or utility, wherein utility meant the potential to improve a decision. What can be deduced from this argument that may shed light on the problem of degrees of accuracy of measurement to which we have earlier referred as a central issue? It appears that a close relationship can apply. If a decision can be made with the same degree of confidence and precision (power) given either $x \pm 5\%$ as with $x \pm 10\%$, then the cost of the reduction of "error" from 10% to 5% is a waste of resources. In such cases the cost of additional accuracy does not result in an increment in the pay-off.

■ *Idle curiosity?*

The criterion to which we have referred each test question has had something to do with the concept of a decision. This is essential. There is no meaning to the concept of "information" except with regard to some external criterion of purpose, some uncertainty. The external criterion may be expressed in probabilistic terms.

We may consider the objection that sometimes the collection of information is carried out only to satisfy "idle curiosity." The test in such cases is the expectation of pay-off in terms of the individual's idiosyncratic behavior. Suppose, for example, that instead of being a person in some authority (in which case the reference base for the pay-off concept is in terms of power) the person requesting the information were a scientist, artist, or "ideas man." If in the past he had shown himself to be a person whose wild ideas had occasionally been extremely fruitful, then the expected utility of the information would not be zero in respect to any future information he might call for. The general principle of inference remains the same whether the decisions are based on research evidence or on the skills of an experienced administrator. It may, moreover, be regarded as most risky, at times, not to take risks. There may be nothing more likely to damage an enterprise than to be unenterprising! It is not the *proof* of utility which is the test, but the *reasonable expectation,* i.e., a probability.

■ *Games and strategy*

The kind of rationale outlined in the previous section is strictly similar whether the method under development is the scientific or administrative. Not all decisions can be made on the basis of scientific evidence, but many of the processes made explicit in terms of the scientific method are learned in the workshop of life in many and various ways by many different kinds of persons. In the immediately preceding example the reader may notice an allusion to concepts used in the theory of games, but people played games for many centuries before there was any theory to match the action. The early Greeks and Romans played games with considerable efficiency, and some well-reasoned strategy is evidenced in their administrative and military operations. Many able administrators of today prefer to refer to examples (models) from those times rather than attempt abstract analysis of the contemporary scene.

It is often difficult to decide whether to refer a particular problem for research, to call for more information, or to accept the existing uncertainty and to make what seems to be the most reasonable decision with the limited set. What information is needed in order to make rational decisions as to whether more information is needed to make the operational decision? This is not a silly question; it is a difficult one. (For discussion of the strategy of social research, see 72, Chapter 5.)

EXPERIENCE TABLES AS INFORMATION

It is, perhaps, rather easy to see how information is related to decisions in the terms described above. It may seem some distance from these operations to the construction of base expectancy tables and their use in evaluation of treatment-punishment decision. But let us consider a simple example of a specific case (we shall add complexity analogous with the evaluation situation as the example develops). Imagine that an employer were about to engage a young worker. His decision is to be made in terms of a simple dichotomy—to engage or not to engage him. Suppose that within the area with which this discussion is concerned, the employer was aware that the applicant had served a sentence in a youth institution, but that this was the only piece of information. Then we would regard the employer as having made the best decision if he were to act *as though* the probability of the applicant's return to crime were the same as the proportion in the total population of the institution—about 50 percent. But suppose that the employer was able to obtain more information, for example, that the applicant had a total of six previous offenses. His action would then be likely to be different from the prior situation where his information was restricted to the simple fact of previous incarceration. His action would then be rational if it were based on these two items of information. In this case the probability of the employee avoiding further convictions would be reduced to about one in three. Similarly each additional piece of information may modify the concept of rational decision according to the greater degree of refinement of estimates of risk. This is in accord with the philosophy of "As If" (64). What, in practice, acting *as if* the applicant had a 50 percent or a 30 percent chance of recidivism might mean (in terms of other decisions), could be dealt with similarly but would render the example highly complex.

We noted in the Introduction that the difference between a "magic" potion and modern medicine did not consist of the chemical composition of the substances but of the relationship between the substances and the outcomes. The need for relevant information, other than information relating to the composition of the substance, is the essential feature. Similarly, when we discussed *information,* we observed that what was and what was not *information* was not a feature of the thing itself, but could be assessed only in terms of a relationship—in this case we proposed the relationship between the *information* and its power to reduce uncertainty in regard to some specific question.

When we say that whether a particular set of operations is or is not treatment depends upon "other relevant established *information*," this phrase has some special meaning. It is not sufficient to say, "I believe that *this is* information," or to say, "I believe that this information is relevant." There is little difference between saying this and saying, "I believe in . . ." whatever form of magic is proposed in the first instance. Thus we are not dealing with separate identities but with relationships, and it is only in the relationships that we can discover any utility.

At some point in any discussion of this kind it is necessary to invoke a belief, if only a belief, that we should be rational beings. The requirement to act or to decide rationally cannot be obtained by means of internal criteria; that is, there is no requirement in rationality itself that it should provide the basis for social action. Nonetheless, most people hold the assumption that we should be as rational as possible.

■ *Adding information and building experience*

If it is accepted that the concept of rationality is related to the concept of use of information, and that both concepts are related to that of utility, then the question of what becomes information is an empirical one related to what it enables us to do. Every item of information tells us something and enables us to do (decide) something that could not be decided (or decided as efficiently) without it. Let us take a piece of information like the example of the employer and the applicant, but let us make this general and refer to the item of information as x_1. This may be the first item of information available, and at this stage we may have only a belief that the item *is* information. We may then test its power to facilitate a decision. If this item shows itself to have any power (*to be information*), then we may seek other information, say x_2. But the selection of item x_1 influences what we can say about x_2 if we propose to use both items. If the addition of x_1 to x_2 does not enable us to do anything more, or more efficiently, than we could with x_1 alone, then x_2 in the presence of x_1 is not information, although it may be information in the absence of x_1. But if x_2

does exist as information in the presence of x_1, then we may combine the two items to assist further in our decisions. But how should these two items be combined? There are many possible systems for combination. If we select one system of combination of $x_1 + x_2$, we may proceed to search for x_3, and the more difficult question then arises as to whether x_3 contributes anything in the presence of $x_1 + x_2$. To some extent this will depend upon the method we selected for the addition of the first two items.

Whether information is processed by the subjective judgment of the individual or by means of mathematical techniques, the same types of problems still apply. We do not know how the human intelligence selects and tests information, and we know even less concerning the human mind's system of combination of complex sets of information. The human intelligence does not seem to be particularly efficient in combining items of information with respect to a particular criterion or task. If we make the combinations by a systematic methodology, at least we shall know what we have done—whether we have added, multiplied, treated as a vector, or the like. The early prediction-table constructors did not work this way. If they found one piece of information that was directly (singly) useful, they retained it and also looked for another by direct tests (singly); if it was independently valuable, they added it to the first. They then similarly looked for a third by independent tests, and when it was found, added it to the two others without testing whether it was of any value in this combined form.

The strategy for utilizing information is, perhaps, one of the more difficult issues both for research and policy. In estimation procedures a degree of control can be exercised; and the criteria for selection, addition, and reduction, can be understood and modified at will.

Each added piece of information must make a contribution to the task (for example, estimation) that has not already been made by other items of information. But complex as this might seem, it is even more complex when it is realized that the sequence in which information is tested may make a difference to the total number of pieces which are eventually put together. Thus, for example, if we start with information about the average duration of an offender's employments and we also note the longest period he stayed in any one job, these two items are so similar to each other that if we choose the former first, when we test the latter it is unlikely to contribute any further information. Similarly, if we test the latter first, then when we test the former it will not contribute anything additional. With these two items this is fairly obvious because the subject to which the information refers is clear. In this instance we might prefer to use the longest period in any one job if it proved as powerful as the average period, since the longest period requires less information to be accurately recorded. But in other cases the link between correlated information may not be obvious; hence, interpretation of equations in any theoretical way is a hazardous procedure.

In this kind of operation (often a form of construction of equations) we do not seek "meaning," whatever that may mean, but rather, efficiency. In the selection of an efficient solution we can follow rules of procedure such that the necessary control is maintained. In the search for more information we have the hard test of use-for-purpose. This is similar to the requirement of sufficient accuracy in regard to single measurements. There is no need to go beyond the point where increased accuracy is of no additional value —that is, where increased information does not add significantly to our ability either to predict or to control. In each case it must be stressed that the specific purpose provides the test. Information that is of no utility for purpose A may be valuable for purpose B, but *there can be no generally useful information,* because we require reference to purpose. Information that has no utility should be rejected from the equations, and we should seek other information as a continuing process so that we continuously reduce the area of our ignorance. We do not accept any abstract theory because it is convincing in itself. We shall decide to accept or reject it after we have investigated those concrete and practical consequences that can be derived from the theory and directly tested.

The search for additional information may be thought of as posing a problem in strategy. Each item of information that can be imagined may be regarded as an applicant for inclusion in any testing analysis. To test its applicability, its suitability for the job, it is necessary to know exactly what that job *is.* Unless the task can be stated for which the information is required, there is little purpose in going further. If the task can be well stated, then there are two further considerations: (1) the expected cost of obtaining the item of information and (2) the cost of testing it. These two items of cost may be compared with the estimated "value." Included in the estimate of value must be some assessment of the probability of its success. An item that would be very "valuable" if it worked, but with only a small probability of working, does not have a high rating of expected utility, particularly if its cost is great. On the other hand, an item that is cheap to collect, even if its probability of success is rated as rather low, might well be a candidate for testing.

Two considerations are necessary in regard to the assessment of the risk in dealing with information: (1) the likely cost of testing the item should it prove useless, and (2) the risk of not testing it should it in fact be useful and its utility remain unknown. Here again are the two classes of error—the producer risk and the consumer risk, or errors of the first and second kind (see Chapter 12).

Social theory provides the best means for the assessment of the likely utility of items of information. Social theory plays its part in the determination of the strategy of social research through the "decision process," which involves the assessment of cost and utility. But in all practical situations there is another factor to be considered in addition to testing costs. At some point, no matter how cheap the information collection and testing procedures may be, the sample size (the body of experience) will become a limiting factor. The cost of increasing the size of the sample to accommodate the testing of further information is a very different matter from the consideration of additional items (noted above). The two factors are not independent, and the nature of the testing strategy is related to the nature of the questions that are the focus of attention. At some point the contribution of any further item of information will become so small in relation to the sample size that it will be impossible to test its significance. Moreover, it is not possible to add "pure" information. For every item of information successfully added, there is also an added element of error. No measurements can be free from variation. Thus it is often desirable to use a strategy of selection that seeks the maximum efficiency with the minimum number of different items of information. By minimizing the number of different items of information, other things being equal, the error is also minimized.

■ *Limitations of experience tables*

Prediction (estimation) methods do not provide a unique solution to any problem, but they can provide a "best" solution, or a "maximum likelihood" solution. The solution obtained in any single case may differ from the solution obtained in another case. Both solutions may be equally as efficient, but the way in which they are composed may be quite dissimilar. The equations provide estimates —that is their job, and for that the method was designed—explanation and interpretation are not the same as estimation.

The search for appropriate information items and ways of combining them is a basic research operation common to many approaches to problem solving, including evaluation studies. Prediction or estimation begins in this way as does most typological analysis. Indeed, the form in which the information is set up for purposes of analysis is similar in appearance—the matrix of correlations or similar coefficients or numbers noting the interrelationships between every item and every other item in the set. For many varieties of analysis even the initial operations are similar; yet within this basis of similarity there are varieties of estimates that can be made, varieties of typologies, varieties of assumptions necessary under different conditions, and so on. It is not possible to generalize about any of these methods. No estimates, typologies, or subdivisions are of any value in themselves; it is the intended action or inference that renders the systems of calculation appropriate or not.

Within any basic set of data it is possible to inhibit certain types of solutions that are not required or to place boundary conditions on the solutions that the analysis might otherwise provide. Prior theoretical or practical considerations may be invoked in deciding which kinds of data should be forced to take a low priority in the combined forms and which might be permitted to receive their full weight. The use of any prepackaged formulae available will result in a half-baked product!

■ *A common method*

The common prediction (probability estimation) approach is to take data contained in files or otherwise known for offenders and to process these data so that the largest proportion of offenders may be correctly classified as either recidivist or not, where this estimate is obtained from an equation of the following form:

$$Y = ax_1 + bx_2 + cx_3 \ldots$$

where Y is a figure representing some score that can be cut at some point to classify the majority of recidivists above the selected value and nonrecidivists below that value. This basic dichotomy may be further subdivided, and it has been found in practice that the higher the score, the greater the probability (frequency) of offenders committing further crimes and being caught within a follow-up period. This is one legitimate way for combining data from the matrix. The results of forms of equations built up on data derived from one sample have been produced in tabulations or curves showing score and probability or risk, or the equations themselves have been modified to yield a direct percentile for expected failure or success. These equations, then, are experience tables. They have been used to predict—that is, they have been assumed to give estimates of the probabilities of recidivism for other offenders from similar populations who have not at the time of observation been exposed to risk of further convictions. This is not an unreasonable assumption provided that conditions remain somewhat constant. These kinds of conditions apply to all experience, whether derived from tabulations and statistical analysis or by subjective assessment.

The method whereby these kinds of tables have been used in evaluation studies is as follows:

1. Information that discriminated between success and failure within the treatment system has been identified.

2. Limiting the information to that available at a certain specific time in the offender's career (for example, immediately before admission to the treatment program), an equation has been fitted to the experience of recidivism in respect to the sample under study (see equation above).

3. Within the above approach, two different approaches have then developed. In some cases these equations have been applied to other samples of persons undergoing treatment in the same general system, and the outcome has been observed and compared with the expected outcome as assessed on the basis of the equations. In other cases the sample has been partitioned and the differences between the expected and observed rates of failure compared.

The validity of any of these methods as procedures for evaluation is limited. There are many questions that cannot be answered by this approach. The power of the basic equation would seem to be critical. If the equations produced at stage 1 are weak, the results of any comparisons will be suspect. In a number of areas it has been impossible to obtain much power in the basic equations. In turn, the power of the equations is related to the amount of heterogeneity or homogeneity of the groups studied. It must be possible to identify the necessary variety in the system; otherwise, assessment is impossible because of the attendant lack of power of discrimination. It is irrelevant whether the lack of variety is due to the fact that the offenders under study are actually similar (how do we know this?) or only appear similar because we cannot describe their differences. Our control of any situation can only be in terms of our model of the situation; what it is in reality will reveal itself partially and gradually as we amend our model.

■ *Variates and attributes*

There are, however, a large number of cases where we know that our model must be inadequate in some respects, but we do not know whether these respects are relevant to any decisions we may make. Perhaps the most notable cases are those in which we have to use our information in terms of attributes or dichotomies, and the information does not in fact come to us in that form. We may have to make weak assumptions regarding types of distributions because we do not know exactly how unsafe more useful assumptions might be. Nonetheless, the mere ability to show that in some respect the model is not a precise mirror of the "real world" does not invalidate operations with the model, unless we can also go on to show a better model for the particular task at hand. For example, there is no way of saying into how many categories the measurement of a man's height should be divided; we only know that no matter how many categories we may use it would be possible to use more and different ones until each was uniquely described to the best of our ability to measure the continuous variable in inches or some other measure. Indeed there is no *general* answer to the question of whether the measurement of height is of any use at all, no matter how few or many categories may be used. The number of categories depends upon the purpose—not the quality of measurement in itself. We may, then, reasonably start with a dichotomy of height into, say, above average and below average, or above 5'7" and below 5'7". There is some general advantage in making the cut in the continuum as near as possible to the center of the distribution in cases where we have no other information leading to a different decision.

OPERATIONAL RESEARCH—CONCLUSION

The field of operational research systems of evaluation is rapidly developing, and further progress will be made if cooperation can be sustained between those who are concerned with social policy and social action and those interested in research methodology.

This may seem a very unsatisfactory manner in which to conclude the discussion of operational research techniques in the evaluation of penal practices. But, at this time, there can be no more satisfactory statement that is also honest. There are so many things that we who have spent many years in research do not know. This ignorance applies to research methods as well as to the area of policy; and, as we have seen, it is not possible to separate these areas of thought and work. There are many methods available, but there are none that are imperative. We can look over our armory of methods in relation to specific problems and make recommendations. We can try to explain what we are doing when we retreat into our models and operate with our particular varieties of symbols. We can emerge from our world of symbols with suggestions. There are many things that *can* be done. Provided that we share the load of doing them with colleagues who have different interests but similar goals, these things may be reasonably well done. But as MacNaughton-Smith (47), remarks in discussing numerical techniques for classification of individuals, "The researcher asks, 'What information should I put in?' and we reply, 'only what you really want to use.'" And elsewhere, "This sounds appallingly subjective, and so it is."

The major outstanding problems, however, are not concerned with *how* to conduct investigations, but with what criteria should be the basis of our evaluation. The research worker is not able to say what *ought* to be done with any greater conviction than anybody else. He may be able to discuss information that may have an impact upon *considerations of what ought to be done* and to indicate what it would probably be necessary to do to *achieve an objective already given.*

The scientist, social policymaker, social worker, politician, and citizen are all part of the same world. All are concerned with the ends desired for society. Today there is no crisis of means; there is a *crisis of purpose.* This applies, perhaps particularly, to our penal

systems; for what defines a society more efficiently than its failures? What better indication of the state of development of a people
than the people it cannot integrate, accommodate, or accept? What
reveals the nature of a society's goals more clearly than the way
it deals with those who fail to achieve them?

||||| 15 |||

Experimental design

This last chapter is intentionally an anticlimax. It does not fit into the scheme of this book as a separate concept but is necessarily involved in principle in what has already been said. Nonetheless, it seems appropriate that some separate and special treatment must be given to the particular methods of data collection and analysis that are termed "experimental." There is, of course, no discrete division between those methods we have termed "operational" and those conventionally known as "experimental." Rather, there are varieties of research designs, the validity of which depends upon the situation as well as the method itself. However, there is one feature that may serve to discriminate between operational and experimental research; the latter term would not be correctly applied to designs that did not include a basic element of randomization. So far, we have referred to these methods only in passing, because of the extreme difficulties usually encountered in attempts to implement them. These difficulties arise from the reluctance of people to perceive the offender as an experimental subject.

The difficulties in obtaining powerful and valid measurement of the variables that we believe to be important make it the more necessary to include within our armory of techniques some which include randomization. There are many problems which are encountered in operational designs which can be avoided by an experimental design in this meaning of the term. Even so, there are further questions that cannot be answered by these methods.

CLINICAL TRIALS

It is interesting that in medicine, where the physical well being of the subject is involved, clinical trials that include randomization have come to be accepted as necessary and moral. However, where the concept of justice is brought into the picture, the idea of experimentation seems foreign in principle to those concerned with administration. Those of us who are concerned with scientific inquiry may disagree with this view of ethical questions, and perhaps our views are conditioned by our knowledge and experience. But we must not be unduly impressed with the easy analogy between medicine and penal treatment because, as has been noted, penal treatment is a complex compounding of activities from which the element of punishment cannot, at this time, be separated.

There are also other difficulties. In clinical trials in medicine, the allocation of patients to a type of treatment or placebo enables evaluation of various treatments to be made because it can be assumed that there will be limited and known interactions. Perhaps if subjects treated with active ingredients discuss their symptoms with placebo-treated subjects, there may be some slight contamination of the data; but the "double-blind" design means that the results cannot be seriously challenged on this score. In penal treatment, however, the interaction between both treatment and subject and between subject and subject is likely to be of significance. The allocation to a treatment type also means allocation to an environment that is not independent of the treatment factors. If persons are allocated at random to treatments T_1, T_2, and T_3, then the persons undergoing these treatments will be a subsample of the total sample subjected to the random allocation. If the basic sample were normally distributed with regard to any parameter (known or unknown), then the subsamples in each treatment would also be normally distributed. This means that in cases where the treatments are institutional, the mixture of offenders to be treated in T1, T2, and T3 will be a heterogeneous group. If, then, part of the effect of treatment is due to peer-group interactions, the random allocation will (in respect of this component) establish exactly similar groups in the different treatments. Purposeful allocation, on the other hand, might reduce the variation within the treatment institutions, but by factors and amounts unknown. The random allocation method does not, as a method, simulate the usual procedures in practice. Because it is our concern to evaluate the practice, some operational elements might well be included in any "experimental design."

Even in medical-clinical trials there are elements that are not dealt with. We are now beginning to see some of the ill effects of too frequent use of antibiotics. This is not because the early experiments were not well designed, but because there are factors that cannot be included in any design. Not only is our knowledge limited in the ultimate, but it is limited in the detail of each particular experiment or operational research investigation. There are many factors that will yield, if at all, only to continuing vigilance. As information increases, so does our power to predict and control; and our power is limited by the scope of our information and the efficiency of our methods of analysis. But no matter how much information we amass and no matter how sophisticated and efficient our use of that information, there will always be gaps and uncertainties. It is never a choice between the ideal and the inferior but between the current and the better. Experimental designs have some advantages over operational designs; and if we can use them, then it might be good strategy to do so. If we cannot use the better designs, then we should use all the information we can handle in the best ways known to us.

A SAMPLE DESIGN

A design of some interest is one that was recently proposed for the New York Division for Youth. It has some qualities of each of the existing methods and represents an approach to evaluation that seems to have much to commend it. Purposeful allocation to the varieties of treatment programs takes place at the same time and in respect to the same treatments as random allocation. Both sets of persons are subjected to careful information-collecting routines while awaiting allocation. In the case of the randomly allocated subjects, this information is not used for allocation but is stored in reserve until completion of the study period. This information can then be invoked to test assumptions regarding the impact of purposeful allocation and the possible effects of factors not included in the design in initial stages. The chart below should prove self explanatory of this two-pronged approach. (See Figure 2.)

The sample design was originally worked out mainly to facilitate the accommodation of moral objections to random allocation to the different forms of treatment. It was believed that some individuals could be harmed if by random allocation they were perchance sent to one of the types of treatment in the experimental system. It is clearly unsatisfactory to attempt any modification to the random allocation for special cases, no matter how small a proportion of the total they may be. If subjective judgment has to be used as a safeguard against allocation to unsatisfactory treatment, then it would have to be used for a group of persons who were distinctly separated from the experimental random allocation group. The accommodation of strong beliefs regarding "possible harm" through inappropriate allocation enables the establishment of replicate treatment groups that are homogeneous, at least in respect to the beliefs of those responsible for allocation. Whether the groups formed from purposeful allocation turn out in fact to be more homogeneous than those where the allocation was random awaits test at the completion of the study. If the two basic subdivisions (random vs. purposeful) show significant differences in outcome, these may be due either to allocation or to the fact that allocation created homogeneity within the groups. The information collected while the individuals awaited allocation (purposeful or otherwise) in the eligible pool can then be used to try to separate out the important features of any differences in relation to success or failure.

The initial collection of information during the eligible pool process is most important, even with designs that may be completely random. There is always a tendency for a system to drift as it becomes more widely known and either more or less acceptable to significant persons in the professions concerned and society at large. The eligible pool information collection provides a monitor on the intake material and hence also provides a monitor for the input decision processes.

One of the difficulties of the prior-probabilities approach to evaluation is the necessity of identifying and collecting a large quan-

FIGURE 2. *Design for a Research Project*

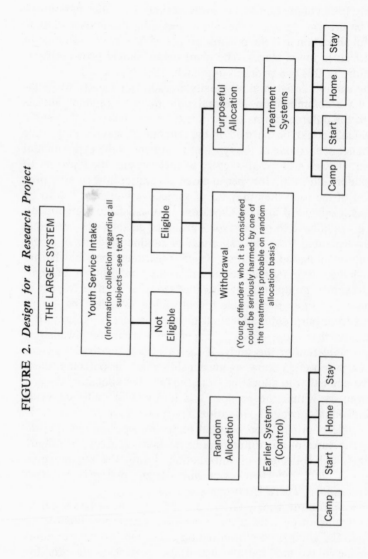

tity of powerful information. The main attraction of the random design has always been that it does not necessitate such careful specification of the variables, because their effects can be neutralized by allocation. This type of design is of particular value in agricultural experiments where many of the variables cannot be modified (e.g., temperature, rainfall, winds) and must be accepted as contributing to "error" variance in terms of measuring types of fertilizer, seeds, and the like. These variables could be very difficult to measure, and measurement would have no purpose because no possible control could be imagined. Hence, they *should* be randomized and neutralized with respect to their effect upon variables that are under control. In these kinds of experiments (the term is here correctly applied) the randomization provides a satisfactory model of the "real" life situation. In the treatment of offenders we cannot be so sure about the nature of the variables, and hence randomization over all but a few selected factors does not provide a satisfactory model. In other words, factorial designs (not to be confused with *factor analysis*) provide a very good experimental situation; data that are powerful are most efficiently used by the system of analysis. Moreover, such experiments can be replicated by other workers—the experimental designs can be related to other experimental designs and the outcomes of similar designs rigorously compared.

RELEVANCE OF REALITY

However, it is unfortunate that the world of human activity is not "designed" like an experimental design! The comparison between two experimental designs may have some value, but at some stage an attempt must be made to relate the internal design to the external world. The utility of the designed experiment depends upon the types of questions that it is reasonable to ask. The relationship between the experimental design and the situations as they affect offenders and those who make decisions about them is always rather tenuous. A large pool of information placed in store at a critical time provides a safeguard for later inference in so many important directions that it should never be overlooked. On the other hand, the need for a pool of information is no excuse for the "magpie method" of investigation where "interesting bits" are assembled, the later utility of which cannot be reasonably justified by some approach to a strategy.

Experimental designs are no panacea for the provision of answers. They afford an important item as a tool of social research and can be fitted into a well-planned general strategy that should also contain the use of simulation and the development of measurement, which includes calculation of estimated probabilities and establishment of typologies.

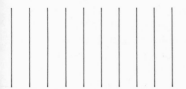

Appendix A:
General prevention measures

There can be little doubt that the way in which offenders are dealt with by the courts affords, in a wide sense, a form of social control. Deterrence of offenders from committing *further* crimes is quite a different matter from the deterrence of *others* from committing crimes in the first instance. In the former case the person who is required to learn conforming behavior is the person directly concerned in the action of society, whereas in the latter case what is done to one person is believed to have an effect upon others.

No scientific policy for dealing with the crime problem should omit consideration of the latter aspects—often termed the "general prevention element."

The majority of people who currently advocate severe punishments usually base their faith in the deterrent effect upon others who might commit offenses rather than upon the reformative or deterrent effect upon the offender himself. This is a difficult hypothesis to test. The problem of deterrence in this form is the problem of normal behavior—why people do not commit crimes or at least avoid getting involved with the formal legal control systems.

The word "deterrence" is itself a term that suggests a pressure toward the commission of crime which is to be offset. It is impossible to define "deterrence" as anything other than a counterforce that makes some sort of balance in a situation which would otherwise be out of balance. It would seem necessary to hypothesize an incentive toward the committing of crime before there can be any meaning in the concept of deterrence to crime. It seems reasonable to suggest that the concept of deterrence has no meaning, nor do the actions developed out of a theory of deterrence have any effect, if there is no need to deter.

It could not be claimed that the average housewife needs to be deterred from poisoning her husband. On the other hand, it might well be sustained that the average motorist needs some deterrence from exceeding the speed limit or taking interesting but unnecessary risks, and there is possibly a need for a deterrent to shoplifting. If these points are admitted, where does the concept of deterrence begin to have meaning? Is it meaningless in relation to serious crimes and meaningful only for petty offenses?

Alternatively, are there *some persons* who are always in need of a deterrent? Should the boundary conditions to deterrence be seen in terms of *persons,* in terms of *events,* or in terms of some compounding of these two dimensions? How is it possible to discuss the concept without reference to some fixed boundary conditions that do not yet seem to have been stated? Clearly no action may be regarded as a deterrent in its own right and in all circumstances. The hypothesis that certain actions will deter in respect of certain people in relation to certain events is more tenable, but the hypothesis contains many unknowns and unestimated limits. Perhaps these unknowns should now begin to be explored.

Of course, if one is talking about the general processes of social controls, then the concept of deterrence in its legal, prohibitive setting becomes a much larger issue and must take into account all the economic, political, social, ethical, and other pressures toward functional behavior—where functional behavior is not necessarily the same as conformist behavior. Indeed, deviant behavior may well be functional for society, but deviant behavior cannot be sanctioned by law. Nor does the law determine the rate of interest, bank rates, terms of credit, and many other social-control systems, except perhaps as the last stage of the process of control when other systems have broken down. Perhaps the concept of deterrence has no meaning unless it is enlarged to mean something quite different from that which it may reasonably be held to mean?

It does not seem unreasonable to propose that before anything may be termed a deterrent to any action, it is necessary to be able to predict that action. Deterrence must relate, if it has any meaning at all, to the inhibition of an event that would otherwise be predicted to happen. Thus, it seems to be a prerequisite of deterrence that human behavior is predictable and that people behave in a somewhat consistent manner, even if not as rational beings. If the behavior of criminals or would-be criminals is totally unpredictable, then no action may be termed a deterrent.

There would seem to be no way of ascertaining whether a person may be expected to be deterred from crime by any particular action, except by means of experimentation. Most arguments, however, are based on the introspection of those concerned or some general theory of needs, drives, or the pleasure-pain principle. It does not seem reasonable to suggest that the views of those of us who have never needed a deterrent are likely to be applicable to those persons for whom we postulate that deterrence is required. The projections of persons who have never really known hunger as to what hungry men might do are not a good basis for estimation. Even the assumption that pain is something to be avoided cannot be applied generally.

There is a large body of psychiatric evidence to support the view that some persons may commit crimes because they *want* to be punished. Would a deterrent in such cases mean the withholding of punishment? The proportion of persons to whom this inversion may apply is doubtless small, but if there is any truth at all in the evidence, it demonstrates that no deterrent is a general one. As soon as the argument of the limitation of the power of any deterrent is accepted, the whole question has to be reexamined. Specific deterrence requires specific or individual prediction. It may be satisfactory to consider deterrence as meaningful with respect only to those *persons* and/or *actions* that can be predicted; otherwise the deterrence may in fact turn out to be an incentive in any one case.

Prediction relies on consistent patterns. It is not far from the concept of consistent behavior to the concept of rational behavior. Whether it is possible for behavior to be consistent and predictable while at the same time it is irrational is not in question here. The problem is whether consistent, irrational behavior (if it exists) could reasonably be expected to be predicted by normal persons using logical processes.

The concept of rational behavior in relation to criminal behavior is also a matter of some difficulty. It seems to follow that the more rational the "criminal," the more "normal" his behavior. Perhaps, therefore, it could be argued that a deterrent could be devised specific to any normal behavior that was rational, and perhaps this concept would include the activities of the so-called professional offender. Most of the public who call for the application of severe deterrent penalties usually desire this in respect to crimes of violence and sex cases. These types of crime would not seem to be reasonably classified as the most "normal" or rational criminal behavior. The public must, of course, be protected from these types of offenses, but it seems improbable that the concept of deterrence is of much assistance here.

Attempts to get money, on the other hand, even if by illegal means, are much more in accord with what is usually perceived as the behavior of rational men.

If the action taken with respect to any individual criminal is to influence the behavior of would-be offenders, it is essential that *information* should be known regarding the situation in which the offender found himself by reason of his action. Indeed, it may be said that if there is any deterrent effect, it is not *what is in fact* done to A which inhibits B but the *information* about it.

It should be noted that in cases of minor offenses and for purposes of some other general social controls, society specifically informs offenders of the likely penalty. For example, the penalty for littering the grass, using an emergency device on a train, and many other such cases is publicized adjacent to the grass, the device, the stop signal, and so on. Thus, the doctrine of deterrence implicitly states that the probability of B committing an offense is changed by his knowledge of what happened to A, but some further links in the chain are still necessary.

It seems that persons concerned in most serious offenses are neither aware of the true probabilities of being caught nor of the likely penalty should they be caught. If there were full knowledge of these necessary facts, would the offender's behavior be different? If different, would there be a lesser or greater likelihood of commission of crime? Perhaps persons are deterred only because their beliefs of what might happen to them are *not* correct. They may tend to overestimate the risk of being caught or the unpleasantness of the likely penalty, or they may have underestimated the gain they thought they might obtain from the crime itself. People's actions are determined by what they believe to be true, not what is in fact true, although changing the facts *may* eventually change the beliefs.

The use of the concept of *information* as a social control, taken in relation with the general preventive aspects of the law, makes it possible to begin stating some meaningful problems in the fields of deterrence that can now be investigated. Until these aspects have been examined, the treatment of offenders must be considered separately from the preventive or deterrent aspects of penal sanctions. The separation of the two aspects is essential before the effects of their interaction may be considered. When we know something about each dimension separately, we may consider how they go together and work toward a rational strategy. Perhaps a suboptimum solution has to be accepted in the one sector due to interaction from the other. This is already becoming evident in some of the developing countries, where the enlightened treatment of youthful offenders is providing better educational facilities than those available to some of the depressed classes who stay on the right side of the law. The treatment, in such cases, may be seen as an incentive to commit crime, not as a deterrent.

Prison communities may be regarded as one-class societies because all prisoners are treated much alike in terms of food, clothing, accommodation, and other social facilities. External societies are not one class, and the amount of deprivation *in* prison will differ according to the class from which the offender comes; thus, the element of punishment in the "same" sentence differs markedly according to the class of the prisoner in the previous environment. Similarly, it would seem necessary to argue that the deterrent effect will differ. Merely to reduce the standard of social facilities in the institution to a point below that of the lowest group outside does not seem to be a solution. The argument sometimes put forward that the institutional standard should be similar to the average in the society (such as nutritional standards and so forth) would mean that for those below average the institutional standards would be higher than those to which they were accustomed. Yet, obviously, treatment concepts require a basic minimum living standard within the institutional setting.

One form of treatment for offenders, and *only* one form, overcomes these problems—treatment within the community.

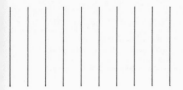

Appendix B:
Morals and models

It has been noted that criminology is conceptually close to ethics; much of the motivation for social action is in good doing. This proximity of value systems to the subject matter of criminology raises problems not encountered in other fields. Certain features of this special relationship differ between different systems of research. We shall explore some aspects of this relationship here.

Throughout this text we have tried to be both cautious and rigorous, and little will be found by way of speculation. We have emphasized the complexity of the problems addressed, and we have noted the need for building complex models to facilitate explanations of observed behavior. Simplification in terms of cryptic summaries was not appropriate. Perhaps, in an appendix some relaxation of these standards may be in order and may even be helpful. First, the summary that follows is intended to be a simplification of the arguments used earlier, and, second, a means of making more explicit some of the assumptions underlying the particular approach adopted throughout. For these reasons, this appendix should be considered in a different light from the other parts of this book, including Appendix A. It is hoped that the following discussion will not be considered irrelevant but instead will prove stimulating.

An attempt has been made to set forth in tabular form a summary of the main differences between the point of view advocated in this work and that of other criminological research workers in the more traditional schools of thought. The viewpoint we have endorsed draws heavily upon the operational (or operations) research methods rather than upon classical research designs. This (and perhaps all attempts to set down the differences in concise terms between research methods without reference to specific instances) means taking risks and inviting criticism. Some criticisms may well concern points of substance, and not all points could be defended under all postulated conditions. Some trade-off is necessary between the need for accuracy (with its attendant complexity) and simplicity of exposition. The attempt is made in the interests of exposition and in the belief that it may clarify some of the rather involved questions raised in an indirect form in the preceding chapters. The differences between the approach advocated in this book and that of many others are not of an all-or-none nature; thus, the phrase "tends toward" has been used in the heading of the tabulation of the columns noting in cryptic form the qualities of the systems.

ROUGH COMPARATIVE MODES OF DIFFERENCE

Classical Research Designs and Criminological Philosophy Tend Toward:	*Systems Advocated in This Book Tend Toward:*
Concepts of truth.	Action that is assessed as rational (strategic) and in accord with an ethic that must be defended.
	Boundary conditions under which decisions are valid.
Internal criteria (e.g., use of factor analysis).	External criteria (e.g., regression analysis and decision models).

Facts.	Acts and reactions.
Absolutes.	Relatives—degrees of belief.
Certainty.	Uncertainty.
Cause and effect.	Probability.
Simple explanations.	Complex explanations.
Grand theories.	Specific theories.
Right vs. wrong (fixed values).	Variable values—situation is relevant to considerations of values.
Can ignore situation as irrelevant, since truth is universal.	Cannot ignore situation, since truth is relevant to the situation.
Assumptions simplified.	Model is simplification of situation; divergence of "map" is discussed as relevant (see below).
Consistent with a *two*-value logic and dichotomies (e.g., guilty or not guilty, responsible or not responsible, true or false, etc.).	Dichotomies may or may not provide an adequate model. Usually dichotomies are seen as a simplification of the situation which may occasionally be justified as a means to provide approximations.
Deterministic philosophy.	Not deterministic, since deterministic models are not usually as powerful as probabilistic models. Does not consider determinism as a significant question or issue at this time.
Nature of the "real" universe is important and is seen as deterministic.	Nature of *model* is important in relation to results derived from its use.
	Strategy of research is decided in terms of prior research results, not by beliefs about a "true" universe.
Reference to some ultimate (e.g., truth) outside the scientist himself.	Reference to our own concept (model) in terms of a democratic authority of the community of scientists.

Data are seen as supporting beliefs of a fairly general kind.	Data are seen as providing information relevant to such further actions as more research action or social policy decisions. However, all results are related to the situation that must be specified. No generalization is expected, although some general qualities may be found.
Hence Since truth can be known, "our" system may be pressed upon others as being "true." (We may identify this tendency as prejudice or dogma.)	Since truth cannot be known (we discuss reasonable decisions under conditions of uncertainty), "our" system may not be the right or best system in other situations. We may not generalize without further support.

There are many other characteristics that could be added to the list to indicate differences in emphasis or tendency and others that are more substantial. However, perhaps enough has been noted to provide a basis for further development and speculation.

Persons who know truths (discovered or revealed) will by this token "know" others to be in error. It is not far from the belief that others are in error to the belief that they must be corrected. This means for correction of others may take the form of missionary zeal, good works, or the inquisition. Whatever the means, they are not regulated by the same processes as those of scientific strategy but would seem to depend only upon the nature of a belief system. This applies whether the truths are revealed or discovered, since once truth is "known," the conditions for its acceptance are no longer in question.

Contrast this view with the one taken in this book. We do not regard it as relevant to ask whether truth exists; it may or it may not, and there is no way for us to know. We make no claims to the discovery of ultimate truth; rather, all "truths" are tentatively held. The models we construct may be sufficient for some purposes and not for others. Often the better models may be those of more general application, but even this point is not one about which we would be dogmatic.

A model may be regarded as something like a map. Maps are of different scales; some scales omit detail because this is the only way to represent the terrain; others give great detail. We select a map according to our purposes, which may be anything from walking to flying, for example. Our models may "map" well or badly on to the situation we are studying, and this feature of "mapping" may be examined. Our information of the world comes to us *through* our maps or models. The reference is not to a belief about what really exists, but is self-centered in terms of our models. We cannot control the "real" world except to the degree that we can control our model of it, and the power of the model depends upon how well or badly it "maps" on to the situation we wish to study.

Is the scientific method, then, all pervasive? This is not the claim. The scientific method is a general feature to be considered, but the scientist's extreme belief that all problems can and should be solved scientifically is as absurd as the extreme administrative view that the "answers are really all so simple." There are administrative prerogatives, and there are always valid moral issues as well as scientific considerations in social policy. The scientist cannot behave as though the moral questions did not arise; similarly, the administrator cannot efficiently carry out his task unless he takes into account the current state of scientific knowledge and its potential. There are many dimensions to all social policy decisions.

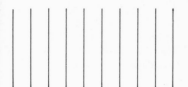

Bibliography and references

Reference
number
in text

Adams, S.   "Some Findings from Correctional Caseload Research" (An-   (1)
aheim: Paper presented at the National Institute of Crime and
Delinquency, 1967).

American Psychoanalytic Association.   "Committees at Work," *Bulletin*   (2)
of the American Psychoanalytic Association, Vol. 6, No. 7, 1950.

Aschaffenburg, G.   *Das Verbrechen und seine Bekampfung,* Heidelberg: (3)
1903.

Bailey, W. C.   "Correctional Treatment: An Analysis of One Hundred   (4)
Correctional Outcome Studies," *Journal of Criminal Law, Crimi-*
nology and Police Science, 57,2 (1966), 153–160.

Baker, F.   *Criminological Prediction: A Comparison of Methods* (tenta-   (5)
tive title). Home Office Research Report. London: H.M.S.O. (to
be published in 1969).

Banks, Charlotte.   Draft research report submitted to Home Office Re-   (6)
search Unit, England (limited circulation; to be published later),
1966.

———.   "Delinquency and Crime," *Proceedings,* Professional Section,   (7)
British Psychological Society. Keele University (mimeo.), 1964.

Beccaria. *An Essay on Crime and Punishment*, 1764.   (8)

Black, B. J., and S. J. Glick. "Recidivism and The Hawthorne-Cedar   (9)
Knolls School." New York: Research Monograph No. 2, Jewish
Board of Guardians, 1952.

Bowman, P. H. "Effects of Revised School Program on Potential   (10)
Delinquents," *Annals*, 322 (1959), 53–62.

Burgess, E. W. "Factors Determining Success or Failure on Parole,"   (11)
in A. A. Bruce, A. G. Haino, and E. W. Burgess (eds.).
The Workings of the Indeterminate Sentence Law of Illinois.
Springfield, Ill.: State Board of Parole, 1928.

Chandler, A., and L. T. Wilkins. "Confidence and Competence in   (12)
Decision-Making," *British Journal of Criminology*, January 1965.

Cloward, R. A., and L. E. Ohlin. *Delinquency and Opportunity.* New   (13)
York: Free Press, 1961.

Cressey, D. "The Nature and Effectiveness of Correctional Techniques,"   (14)
Law and Contemporary Problems, 23 (1956), 754–771.

———. "Contradictory Theories in Correctional Group Therapy Pro-   (15)
grams," *Federal Probation*, 18 (1954), 20–26.

Criminal Statistics. Annual publication of Home Office, England and   (16)
Wales. London, H.M.S.O.

Denker, P. G. "The Prognosis of Insured Neurotics," *New York State*   (17)
Journal of Medicine, 37 (1937), 238.

Ernst, K. *Über Gewalttätigkeitsverbrecher Und Ihre Nachkommen.*   (18)
Berlin, 1938.

Eysenck, H. "The Effects of Psychotherapy—An Evaluation," *Journal*   (19)
of Consultive Psychiatry, 16 (1952).

Fisher, R. A. *Design of Experiments.* London: Oliver and Boyd, 1935.   (20)

Freedman, R. "Incomplete Matching and Ex Post Facto Designs,"   (21)
American Journal of Sociology, 55 (March 1950), 485.

Frey, E. "Der Frühkriminelle Rückfallsverbrecher. Criminalite Precoce   (22)
et Recidivisme," *Schweizerische Criminalistiche Studien*, 4, Basel:
Verlag Für Recht und Gessellschaft, 1951.

Gersten, C. "An Experimental Evaluation of Group Therapy with   (23)
Delinquents," *International Journal of Group Psychotherapy*, 1
(1951), 311–318.

Glaser, D. *The Effectiveness of a Prison and a Parole System.*   (24)
Indianapolis: Bobbs-Merrill, 1964.

———. "Criminality Theories and Behavioral Images," *American*   (25)
Journal of Sociology, 61 (1956), 433–444.

Glueck, E., and S. Glueck. *Five Hundred Criminal Careers.* New York: (26)
Knopf, 1930.

———. *Later Criminal Careers.* New York: The Commonwealth Fund;   (27)
London: H. Milford, Oxford University Press, 1937.

———. *Criminal Careers in Retrospect.* New York: The Common-   (28)
wealth Fund, 1943.

———. *Unravelling Juvenile Delinquency.* New York: The Common-   (29)
wealth Fund, 1950.

Grant, J. D., and M. Q. Grant. "A Group-Dynamics Approach to the (30) Treatment of Non-Conformists in the Navy," *Annals,* 322 (1959), 126–135.

Grant, J. D. "It's Time to Start Counting," *Crime and Delinquency,* (31) 8 (1962), 5.

Grassberger, R. *Die Losung Kriminalpolitisher.* Vienna, 1946. (32)

Hammond, W. H., and E. Chayen. *Persistent Criminals.* A Home (33) Office Research Unit Report. London: H.M.S.O., 1963.

Hart, H. "Predicting Parole Success," *Journal of Criminal Law and* (34) *Criminology,* 14 (1923), 414–425.

Healy, W. *The Individual Delinquent.* Boston: Little, Brown, and (35) Co., 1915.

Kingston, C. R. "Applications of Probability Theory in Criminalistics," (36) *Journal of the American Statistical Association,* 60, 1965.

Kirby, B. C. "Measuring the Effects of Treatment of Criminals and (37) Delinquents," *Sociology and Social Research,* 38 (1954), 368–374.

Kobrin, S. "The Chicago Area Project: A Twenty-five Year Assess- (38) ment," *Annals of the American Academy of Political and Social Science,* 322 (1959), 20.

Kogi, S., Y. Ishikawa, and J. Sugamata. Fuchu, Tokyo, Japan: United (39) Nations Asia and Far Eastern Institute for the Treatment of Offenders, 1966 (translated mimeograph).

Lenz, A. *Grundriss Der Kriminalbiologie.* Vienna, 1927. (40)

Levitt, E. E. "The Results of Psychotherapy with Children: An Evalua- (41) tion," *Journal of Consultive Psychiatry,* 21 (1957), 189.

Lombroso, C. *Crime, Its Causes and Remedies.* H. Horton (trans.). (42) Boston: Little, Brown, and Co., 1911.

Lotz, L. *Der Getfahrliche Gewohnheitsvekbrecher.* Leipzig, 1939. (43)

Mann, A. "Group Therapy," *Journal of Criminal Law and Criminology,* (44) 46 (1955), 50–66.

Mannheim, H., and L. T. Wilkins. *Prediction Methods in Relation to* (45) *Borstal Training.* London: H.M.S.O., 1955.

McClintock, F. H., M. A. Walker, and N. C. Savill. *Attendance Centers.* (46) London: Macmillan, 1961.

MacNaughton-Smith, P. *Some Statistical and Other Techniques for* (47) *Classifying Individuals.* London: H.M.S.O., Codes 34–368–6, 1965.

———, and L. T. Wilkins. "New Prediction and Classification Methods (48) in Criminology," *Journal of Research Crime and Delinquency,* 1 (1964), 19–32.

Meehl, P. *Clinical vs. Statistical Prediction.* Reprint, 1966. University (49) of Minnesota Press, 1954.

Metfessel, M. and C. Lovell. "Recent Literature on Individual Corre- (50) lates of Crime," *Psychological Bulletin,* March 1942.

Metzger, E. *Kriminologie.* Munich, 1951. (51)

Nakata, I., and S. Okusawa.   Translation from Japanese, United Nations   (52)
Asia and Far East Institute, Papers. Tokyo, 1965.

Powers, E., and H. Witmer.   *An Experiment in the Prevention of*   (53)
Delinquency. New York: Columbia University Press, 1951.

Reed, E. F.   "How Effective Are Group Work Agencies in Preventing   (54)
Juvenile Delinquency," *Social Service Review,* 22 (1948), 341–
348.

Roman, M.   *Reaching Delinquents through Reading.* Springfield, Ill.:   (55)
Thomas, 1957.

Saslow, G., S. Saslow, *et al.*   "A Follow-up Study of Untreated Patients   (56)
with Various Behavioral Disorders," *Psychiatric Quarterly,* 30
(1956), 238–302.

Schnell, Karl.   *Anlage und Unwelt Bei 500 Ruckfallsuerbrechern.*   (57)
Leipzig, 1935.

Schulman, H. M.   "Delinquency Treatment of the Controlled Activity   (58)
Type," *American Sociological Review,* 10 (1945), 405–414.

Schurich, J.   *Lebenslaufe Vielfach Ruckfalliger Verbsrecher.* Leipzig,   (59)
1930.

Stott, D. H.   "Prediction from Non-Delinquent Behavior," *British*   (60)
Journal of Criminology, January 1960.

The Sentence of the Court, Home Office Report. London: H.M.S.O.,   (61)
Code 34–433–0–66, 1964.

Thomas, W. I.   "The Behavioral Pattern and the Situation," *American*   (62)
Sociological Society Publication, 22 (1927), 1–13.

Tufts, E., and H. L. Witmer.   "The Effectiveness of Delinquency Pre-   (63)
vention Programs." Washington, D.C.: U.S. Department of
Health, Education, and Welfare, Children's Bureau, 1954.

Vaihinger.   *The Philosophy of "As If."* C. K. Ogden (trans.). London: (64)
K. Paul; New York: Harcourt, 1924.

Vold, A. B.   *Prediction Methods and Parole.* Hanover, N.H.: Sociolog-   (65)
ical Press, 1936.

Wallerstein, S. B.   "Comparative Study of Treatment Methods for   (66)
Chronic Alcoholism," *American Journal of Psychiatry,* 113
(1923), 228–235.

Walters, A. A.   "A Note on Statistical Methods of Predicting De-   (67)
linquency," *British Journal of Criminology,* 4, 1955–1956.

Warner, S. B.   "Factors Determining Parole for the Massachusetts   (68)
Reformatory," *Journal of Criminal Law and Criminology,* 14
(1923), 172–207.

Weeks, H. Ashley.   *Youthful Offenders at Highfields.* Chicago: Univer-   (69)
sity of Chicago Press, 1958.

Wend, J.   *Untersuchungen an Straflisten Vielfach Ruckfalliger Ver-*   (70)
brecher. Leipzig: Wiegandt, 1936.

Wilkins, L. T.   "Information and Decisions Regarding Offenders," in   (71)
S. A. Yefsky, *Law Enforcement, Science and Technology.* Washington: Thompson, 1967.

————. *Social Policy, Action, and Research.* Social Science Paperback, (72)
No. 7. London, Tavistock, 1967.

————. "New Thinking in Criminal Statistics," *Journal of Criminal* (73)
Law, Criminology, and Police Science, 56 (1965), 3.

Witmer, H., and E. Powers. *An Experiment in the Prevention of De-* (74)
linquency. New York: Columbia University Press, 1951.

Wootton, B. *Social Science and Social Pathology.* London: Allen and (75)
Unwin, 1957.

Yates, F. *Sampling Methods for Census and Survey.* London: Griffin, (76)
1953.

Index

About the author

Leslie T. Wilkins was born in Colchester, England, in 1915. Educated in England, he was a statistician in the British Civil Service for several years and was later a senior advisor for the United Nations. He has served on the President's Committee on Youth Crime, acted as a consultant for the Department of Corrections and Youth Authority of California, and was a consultant to the President's Commission on Law Enforcement and Administration of Justice, as well as several other state, national, and international consultative committees. Mr. Wilkins has published extensively in journals, has written six books, including *Social Deviance* (1964), and has contributed chapters to several books. He is currently a professor and acting dean in the School of Criminology at the University of California, Berkeley. He is married and has four children.

A note on the type

The text of this book was set on the Linotype in a face called
Times Roman, designed by Stanley Morison for *The Times* (London),
and first introduced by that newspaper in 1932.

Among typographers and designers of the twentieth century,
Stanley Morison was a strong forming influence, as typographical advisor
to the English Monotype Corporation, as a director of two distinguished
English publishing houses, and as a writer of sensibility, erudition,
and keen practical sense.

Composed, printed, and bound by The Colonial Press, Clinton, Mass.